D1351482

BASIC BOOKS IN EDUCATION

Editor: *Kathleen O'Connor, B.Sc., Senior
Lecturer in Education, Rolle College, Exmouth*
Advisory Editor: *D. J. O'Connor, M.A., Ph.D.,
Professor of Philosophy, University of Exeter*

Philosophy and Education: An Introduction

This book provides an introduction to the philosophy of education for those with no previous knowledge of philosophy. The approach is analytic (for example, the author describes what we mean by 'education', 'knowledge', 'teaching' and 'learning'); but the book also presents a systematic account related to the actual situation in schools. Particular attention is paid to questions about knowledge and, although no attempt is made to discuss the problems of value judgements, the way in which such judgements affect words like 'education' and 'teaching' is discussed. The author also stresses the educational importance of the first acquisition of concepts and language and the fact that much of the education of the child takes place outside school.

Key words in the text are in SMALL CAPITALS, there are summaries and 'further reading' lists at the end of each chapter and there is a full bibliography, glossary and index.

Philosophy and Education: An Introduction

GLENN LANGFORD, B.A., B.Sc. (Econ.)
LECTURER IN PHILOSOPHY AT THE
UNIVERSITY OF EXETER

MACMILLAN
London · Melbourne · Toronto
1968

TO DAVID, JULIET AND SALLY

© Glenn Langford 1968

Published by
MACMILLAN AND COMPANY LTD
Little Essex Street London W C 2
and also at Bombay Calcutta and Madras
Macmillan South Africa (Publishers) Pty Ltd Johannesburg
The Macmillan Company of Australia Pty Ltd Melbourne
The Macmillan Company of Canada Ltd Toronto

Printed in Great Britain by
ROBERT MACLEHOSE AND CO LTD
The University Press, Glasgow

Contents

Acknowledgments

A book of this sort necessarily relies heavily on the work of others. Some indication of the extent of my indebtedness is given by the Bibliography. I should like to acknowledge a particular debt to those who taught me at Birkbeck College; to discussions with colleagues at Exeter; and to the editors, Professor D. J. and Kathleen O'Connor, for their detailed and helpful criticism.

I should also like to thank the following for their kindness in giving permission for the use of copyright material: George Allen & Unwin Ltd., for an extract from *Principia Ethica*, by G. E. Moore; George Allen & Unwin Ltd. and The Macmillan Company, New York, for extracts from *Logic and Knowledge*, by Bertrand Russell; Professor A. J. Ayer, for the extract from *The Problem of Knowledge*; and Scott, Foresman & Company, for the extract from *Conditions of Knowledge*, by Israel Scheffler: © Scott, Foresman & Co. 1965.

1 Philosophy of Education

1 EDUCATION AS AN ACTIVITY

Most people know what education is because they have had direct experience of it; but of course it doesn't follow that they can *say* what it is. But at least everybody would agree that it has got something to do with what goes on in schools, colleges and universities; and this will do for a start.

The point of what goes on in schools is that somebody should become educated. For the moment I am not concerned with what it is to become educated; but simply to point out that education is an activity which aims at a practical result. Children go to school to get educated and teachers go to educate them. So if we ignore for the moment *what* the practical result is, education can be compared to other activities which also aim at a practical result. In some cases it is easy enough to say what result is aimed at; manufacturers make things, tangible things like motor cars and washing machines; farmers grow food, like wheat and prime beef. In other cases, like politics, a brief statement of the practical result aimed at seems to leave out most of what we want to know; it is no more helpful to say that politics aims at running the country than it is to say that education is concerned with educating people. It is therefore not coincidence that politics has attracted even more philosophical interest than education.

Activities which are practical in the sense in which I have been trying to explain I will call PRACTICAL ACTIVITIES. But not all activities in which people engage are practical in this sense. They are not practical because they are not concerned to change anything; rather they are concerned to discover what is the case. Of course you have got to do something to discover what is the case – if it is only looking at the clock to see what time it is. But this is different from winding up the clock to make sure it goes, or so that you can hear the tick. And when such THEORETICAL ACTIVITIES become highly organised and specialised we speak of the theoretical disciplines of physics, psychology, and so on. Such activities are theoretical in the sense that they are concerned with truth rather than change. Of course, discoveries in particular theoretical disciplines are not wholly unrelated to change; indeed they create new possibilities of change. It is for this reason that hard-headed business men are prepared to finance research; the Bell Telephone Laboratories provide an outstanding example. And in the next section I shall consider the relationship between the practical activity of those engaged in education and the possibilities of change opened up by theoretical knowledge.

Before doing so, I ought to point out that education is connected with knowledge in a second way. Whereas the car manufacturer uses knowledge in order to make cars, those engaged in education use knowledge in order to pass knowledge on. The nature of this connection between education and knowledge will be explored in detail later; for the moment it represents something of a digression.

2 EDUCATIONAL PROBLEMS

'Education' then is the name of a practical activity, like farming or gardening; it is not the name of a theoretical activity like physics or psychology.

Those who engage in such an activity will rely, in the first instance, on the traditional way of doing things. How things are done at present offers the most obvious guide to the way to do them in the future. But departures from the traditional way may become possible or desirable for a number of reasons. New knowledge may open up new possibilities; new building methods, for example, have been made possible by the invention of structural steel. And even without the advent of new knowledge, reflection may suggest that existing methods of doing things are not the best currently available; existing knowledge is seldom fully utilised. Or circumstances may change and force the conclusion that existing practice is no longer adequate or acceptable.

A change in the ratio of teachers to pupils due to a rise in the birth rate or a failure in teacher-recruiting might be one such circumstance. Or moral attitudes may change, as they did when pit managements were forced to replace children by ponies to haul coal.

So education may be regarded as an activity which presents problems to those engaged in it; either because of dissatisfaction with existing practice or because situations arise to which existing practice offers no ready answer. How are such problems to be met?

A rational, as opposed to an arbitrary, solution will be one which is adopted because there are good reasons for doing so; it will also, therefore, be one which can be defended or justified by pointing to those reasons. Good reasons are those which might be expected to command acceptance in a public debate; the purely personal preferences of particular individuals do not, therefore, provide acceptable grounds for the adoption of a solution to a problem involving the interests of others.

More positively, what constitutes a good reason for adopting a particular answer to a problem arising in a practical activity such as education? How is the worth of reasons put forward to be assessed?

(a) Reasons must be relevant to the problem in hand. The relevance of a reason can only be judged by those who have a detailed knowledge of the activity and can therefore understand the context within which the problem is seen as a problem. Such understanding will involve not only factual knowledge of the educational set-up; but also a realisation of the point of the activity (i.e. an understanding of what is involved in becoming educated).

(b) Many of the reasons offered rely on the findings of particular theoretical disciplines, such as psychology, sociology and economics. To assess the worth of these reasons it is essential to look to the correct theoretical discipline. It is the business of the psychologist, for example, to distinguish between those psychological beliefs which are well-founded and those which are not; and to do this a host of experimental and statistical techniques have been devised. Often the psychological evidence is non-existent or inconclusive; either because the relevant research has not been undertaken or because it has so far failed to produce any positive results.

(c) Given knowledge of the existing situation, and the possibilities of change available, we still have to decide whether a particular change is desirable. Some, and often the main, arguments for or against a proposed change will be moral arguments. It is especially important that moral arguments should be identified as such. This is because there are special difficulties involved in distinguishing, or attempting to distinguish, between correct and incorrect moral judgments. Indeed, some philosophers have suggested that this distinction cannot be made at all in the field of morals. These questions are discussed in detail in a separate volume in this series. But what at least is obvious is that the way a moral opinion is to be justified – if justification is possible at all – is different from the way a psychological opinion is to be justified.

(d) Any attempt to solve a problem presupposes an adequate understanding of what that problem is. This involves not only the factual knowledge stresses in (a) above, but also an understanding of the language in which the problem is described and the arguments for or against possible solutions presented. Since such problems arise in the context of the practical activity of education, part of what is required is an understanding of the language of education. Indeed, one way of trying to understand the point of that activity (also stressed in (a) above) is by considering what we are saying when we talk of education. And in so far as the arguments for or against possible solutions to them rely on the findings of particular theoretical disciplines, an understanding of the language used in those disciplines is also necessary.

(e) Arguments typically pass from premises (which are taken as true) to conclusions which follow from those premises, and which are therefore also accepted as true. Someone may, however, claim that a conclusion follows from certain premises, when it does not in fact do so. Logic is the branch of philosophy which specially concerns itself with the rules to which arguments must conform if they are to be valid.

3 SOME EXAMPLES OF EDUCATIONAL PROBLEMS

The main point I have been trying to establish is that educational problems come to us wearing no label except 'educational'; and that this label reflects only their common origin in the practical activity of education. The justification of particular practices, or the arguments for particular changes, look not to one but to a variety of sources. Decisions, if they are rational, will be based on reasons; but reasons are not all of a kind.

Consider, first, an incident which might occur in a classroom; a teacher hits a boy on the head with a steel rule and causes an open wound. Such an incident can be considered from a variety of points of view:

legal – 'old Smithy has laid himself wide open – a good job the parents don't bother.' (The last part of this remark goes beyond consideration of the legal implications of the situation; it relies on local knowledge to conclude that legal redress is not in fact likely to be sought.)

moral – 'even if he gets away with it, he shouldn't have done that.'

psychological – 'you won't get him to learn arithmetic that way' (or, depending on your view of the psychological evidence, 'that's the way to knock it into their heads').

economic – 'if skilled teachers did not have to spend their time and energy just keeping children under control, they could get on with the teaching job they were trained to do'. (Or perhaps, 'if teachers took better note of psychological findings (or if more money were spent on obtaining such findings) their efforts would be more productive').

Of course the obvious way to view such an incident is the second – the moral one; and the comment made there is probably the most important one to make about such an incident. But the point of offering the example is that other, quite distinct, remarks can be made even about an incident like this.

The position is similar if what is in question is the adoption of some general practice; we need at least to be clear on the sort of grounds on which a policy is recommended. *Non-streaming in junior schools* may be defended by suggesting that all children, or perhaps the duller ones, will benefit academically. The grounds for such a suggestion would be primarily psychological. Children differ in their capacity to learn, due to differences in ability and attitude; and recognition of this rules out class-teaching methods. And in an unstreamed class such differences become so glaring that the teacher is forced to teach each child individually. In assessing such a suggestion, therefore, one would have to consider the evidence for supposing that children of the same age do differ widely in their capacity to learn, as well as such detailed circumstances as size of classes, ability and training of teachers, and size of classrooms. But all this is beside the point if the real reason for wanting unstreamed classes is that it is socially undesirable to segregate children on the basis of academic ability. The position is similar to the controversy over comprehensive schools; the case is often argued in terms of A-level results and university places gained. But comparisons with grammar schools on these grounds are largely irrelevant if what one is really interested in is the production of a socially integrated society.

Autistic children are extremely withdrawn, and unresponsive to approaches made to them by others, including parents and teachers. Could not the methods which psychologists rely on in training rats to run mazes and press levers be applied here? Rats are unlikely to learn to run a maze for a food reward if they are not hungry; they are therefore primed for an experimental session by being deprived of food for a period, twenty-four or forty-eight hours, before an experiment. Might not autistic children also learn certain things – if only to make some response to the presence of the teacher – if they are starved and then offered food rewards for doing so? Such a procedure might be challenged by pointing out that it wouldn't work; but even if it did it is obvious that it might be challenged on other grounds, grounds which are not psychological at all but moral.

In these two examples I have considered mainly the possibility that an education problem should be seen as wearing the label 'psychological', so leading to the neglect of other aspects of the problem, in particular the moral aspect. In particular, the danger is that psychological evidence should be taken as supporting a moral point of view. But there is also a possibility that preoccupation with the moral aspects of a problem may lead to a neglect of psychological considerations.

Self-discipline. Most people would agree that self-discipline is preferable to discipline imposed from without; and this is clearly a moral preference. But it does not follow from this alone that a secondary modern school in a tough area should be run (or rather attempted to be run) without any reliance on external discipline. There is no psychological evidence whatsoever that self-discipline is to be produced by the wave of a wand or by fiat; self-discipline does not automatically result simply because external discipline is removed.

In other cases the ambiguity of the language in terms of which a problem is conceived make it difficult to separate psychological and moral considerations. It then becomes necessary to pay careful attention to the language in terms of which the problem is expressed.

Maladjusted children. Children whose behaviour is grossly anti-social, and who are difficult to handle in a normal class-room, are often referred to as maladjusted; and special educational provision is made for them. And it is argued that, since they are the victims of psychological and social circumstances, rather than just naughty, they cannot help what they do and should not, therefore, be punished. The conclusion that they should not be punished is taken to be supported by the psychological evidence of their special difficulties. But the decision to withdraw responsibility for their actions from such children is a moral one; and not only a moral one, but a drastic one. If taken seriously it not only precludes any possibility of effective teaching, but also denies to such children the status of responsible human beings; they are morally degraded in the most literal sense. This conclusion could be avoided if 'maladjusted' is taken simply to refer to a psychological diagnosis, referring to the special difficulties which some children have in conforming to the standards of behaviour laid down in an ordinary school. The way is then open for a very much less drastic proposal: that the standards at special schools should be adjusted in accordance with the personality difficulties of those to whom they will apply. Children would then still be held responsible for breaches of them; though, as is normally the case, responsibility for such breaches would be mitigated by special circumstances.

In these examples I have focused attention on the moral and psychological aspects of educational problems, but my main point is that educational decisions will be based, not on one or two, but on a variety of sorts of considerations. Teaching machines or television, for example, may be effective teaching aids, but be hopelessly expensive. And, at whatever age children become ready for school, the law says they start at five, and until it is changed, what the law says is the first consideration.

4 PHILOSOPHY OF EDUCATION

It follows from what I have said that education does not form a subject of study in the same way as particular theoretical disciplines like psychology or physics or economics. In so far as there is such a subject its unity is provided by the problems and practices of those engaged in education. Teachers and educational administrators, and indeed any who take a serious interest in education, will certainly need to form some sort of synoptic view. They will want to have informed views on education and will, therefore, look to psychology and other subjects for any findings which may be relevant. No one else can provide such a synopsis for them; it is certainly not the job of the philosopher to do this. But the philosopher may provide his own contribution to the formation of such informed points of view.

Philosophy of education, then, is not an independent subject; it is not just a pretentious name for theory of education, for there is no such subject. Rather it just is philosophy, but with an eye to the practices and problems of those engaged in or concerned with education; just as the psychology of education is simply those parts of psychology which are relevant to education. Of course, the findings of educational psychology, educational sociology, philosophy of education, economics of education and so on need to be reconciled and synthesised; but to do so is not to engage in an independent theoretical discipline, but to engage in the solution of educational problems or to acquire informed opinions about such problems.

Philosophy cannot, therefore, by itself provide any answers to educational problems, but neither can any other theoretical discipline. But examination of the language of education, in terms of which those problems are formulated, will help make clear what those problems are, and draw attention to the sort of evidence which is relevant to their solution. G. E. Moore, in the Preface to *Principia Ethica*, points out that many of the difficulties and disagreements in ethics 'are mainly due to a very simple cause: namely to the attempt to answer questions, without first discovering what question it is which you desire to answer'; and this remark applies equally to education.

In this book, however, I shall not be concerned with particular educational problems but with the general context in which they occur. What, in general, are those engaged in education doing? What is it to educate or to become educated? Such an enquiry is important, I think, in two ways. Firstly, the discussion of particular educational problems will be more profitably undertaken in the context of an understanding of education as a whole. I suggested earlier (2a above, p. 9) that the relevance of reasons to problems could only be judged in the light of both knowledge of the details of the situation and a realisation of the point of the activity as a whole. This, I think, is what lies behind the frequent demand for clarification of the aims of education; and I will discuss this demand in detail in a later chapter. But secondly, and in a way more important, I think such an understanding is important for its own sake, and would be important even if it contributed nothing to educational change. It is true that philosophy of education would then be of no use, in the sense of not being instrumental in the production of something else that we want. But it might, nevertheless, be useful in the more important sense of being one of the things that we want. Certainly there must be some things which we want for themselves if there are to be other things which we want as means to them.

I think, therefore, that philosophy can help to provide a clearer understanding of what they are doing on the part of those actively engaged in education. Not everybody will share this marked preference for knowledge over ignorance, for self-knowledge over unthinking performance of routine, but it is reasonable to hope that teachers, at least, will do so. Bertrand Russell puts the point better than I can hope to do:

Philosophy is not a short cut to the same kind of results as those of other sciences. If it is to be a genuine study, it must have a province of its own, and aim at results which the other sciences can neither prove nor disprove. Consequently, we must renounce the hope that philosophy can promise satisfaction to our mundane desires. What it can do, when it is purified of all practical taint, is to help us to understand the general aspects of the world and the logical analysis of familiar but complex things. . . . But a genuine scientific philosophy cannot hope to appeal to any except those who have the wish to understand, to escape from intellectual bewilderment.

I think it is fair to point out that those who do not have the wish to understand, or to escape from, intellectual bewilderment, are at best only passengers in the business of education.

SUMMARY

1. Education is activity, like politics, manufacturing or farming, which aims at a practical result. A practical activity may be contrasted with a theoretical activity which is concerned to discover how things are; physics and psychology are examples.

2. Those engaged in education face practical problems to which definite answers have to be provided. A rational, as opposed to an arbitrary, solution to those problems will be based on a variety of reasons and in assessing the worth of reasons put forward it is vital to look to the correct theoretical discipline.

3. Educational problems have in common only their origin in the practical activity of education. Examination of educational problems shows that the grounds on which particular policies are advocated are not all of a kind.

4. Actual decisions must be based on all the relevant reasons, but no formal guidance can be provided as to how the necessary synoptic point of view is to be achieved. Certainly philosophy can provide no such guidance. But philosophy can make its own contribution: firstly, by an examination of the language of education, making possible a clear formulation of the problems to be solved; secondly, and again by the way of the examination of language, helping those engaged in education to achieve a clearer understanding of just what they are doing.

FURTHER READING

1. Oakeshott (chapter 5 of 59; also chapter 1 of 50) discusses politics as an empirical activity.

2. Weldon (104, especially chapters 1 and 5) stresses the importance of intensive study of the facts in arriving at solutions to practical problems. Weldon (104, chapter 2) and Oakeshott (59, especially chapters 1 and 3) both deny, though for different reasons, an independent role for principles in making practical decisions. See also Berlin (51, chapter 1), Griffiths (113) and Winch (106, pages 54–64).

On the importance of the point of a practical activity, see (121).

For a short introduction to symbolic logic, see (9).

4. Hirst (115) discusses the relationship between philosophy and educational theory in some detail. See also O'Connor (61, especially chapter 5) and Peters (72, Introduction).

On activities undertaken for their own sake, see MacIntyre (46, chapter 1), Weldon (104, chapter 5, section 3), Oakeshott on a self-moved manner of activity (50, chapter 1) and Peters (72, Part One, and 71).

The quotation from Russell is from Russell (82, pages 28–9).

2 Philosophy

The philosopher's contribution to the understanding of educational problems and practice will, I have suggested, be made through the consideration of language. A careful regard for the subtleties of language is by no means new in philosophy, but it is only in the present century that philosophers, or at least British and American philosophers, have become so preoccupied with language. Some explanation of this needs to be offered if philosophy is not to be dismissed as trivial and the philosopher accused of concerning himself with the shadow rather than the substance. After all, someone who is interested in children is interested in boys and girls, flesh and blood creatures who may be happy or unhappy, loved or uncared for, or taught well or badly. He is not interested in the word 'children', which may be typed or written, spelt correctly or incorrectly, or translated into French, but which certainly cannot be happy or unhappy.

There are, of course, good reasons for the linguistic trend in philosophy, but they are essentially philosophic reasons and a proper appreciation of them would be a product of a study of philosophy rather than a preliminary to it. In the same way, a great deal of modern experimental psychology seems trivial to the casual observer, and to understand fully just what psychologists are doing, and why they consider that what they do is worth doing, is to be a psychologist. While, therefore, the question 'Why should I, as a teacher, concern myself with philosophy?' is a natural one to ask, it is also difficult to answer. The only proper answer is 'Do some philosophy, and then judge for yourself'; and I hope that this book will provide a limited opportunity for doing just that, and that the references given will provide a more extended opportunity for doing so. The most I can hope to do in the present chapter is provide some general remarks by way of introduction.

2 THE TRADITIONAL ROLE OF PHILOSOPHY

I want to try to give some explanation of why philosophers have come to concern themselves so much with language. In order to do this I will first try to identify what I will call the traditional role of philosophy. It is true that prior to the twentieth century philosophers did not often have much to say about what they took themselves to be doing; they took it for granted that philosophy was important and that they knew what its job was. Often, too, the people we think of as the great philosophers of the past were interested in many other things and did not draw a sharp line between their philosophical thought and their thought on other matters. Nor can all the philosophic thought of the past be made to fit into one mould. But, bearing in mind all these qualifications, it is possible to attempt a rough characterisation of what philosophers have traditionally taken themselves to be doing; i.e. something like:

giving an account of the world in the most general possible terms;

giving an account of reality (that is, of the real world, as opposed to the world of appearance);

giving an account of the world and man's place in it.

To give such an account is to engage in METAPHYSICS. Metaphysical speculation is certainly not the only activity in which philosophers have engaged in the past, but I think it is fair to say that it is what they have regarded as most important. F. H. Bradley, in the Introduction to *Appearance and Reality*, first published in 1893, suggests that we may agree 'to understand by metaphysics an attempt to know reality as against mere appearance, or the study of first principles or ultimate truths, or again the effort to comprehend the universe, not simply piecemeal or by fragments, but somehow as a whole'.

To understand fully what is being said here one would need

to go on to see what such an attempt looked like. In Bradley's case, this would involve reading the five hundred pages of *Appearance and Reality*; preferably turning also to the two-volumed *Principles of Logic* for fuller understanding. But the characterisations given above at least make it clear why EPISTEMOLOGY (theory of knowledge) has traditionally occupied a position of central importance, alongside that of metaphysics, in philosophy. Epistemology is concerned with knowledge, and what is known to be the case (really known, not just claimed to be known) *is* the case. Hence one who has knowledge knows what the world is really like. Philosophers have, therefore, taken very seriously those who have doubted whether knowledge is possible. 'How do we know that what we take to be knowledge really is knowledge and not just opinion?'; 'Is there any infallible method of obtaining knowledge?'; and, of course, 'What is knowledge?' are the sort of questions which have been considered in epistemology. But on the traditional view of philosophy, what is taken as of primary importance is the subject-matter of philosophy, i.e. the world, or reality, or the universe as a whole. Questions of method, by contrast, are secondary; it has often been supposed, for example, that only if the right method is followed is knowledge possible. What is sometimes called the EMPIRICIST tradition suggests that only through the evidence of our senses is knowledge of the world possible; the RATIONALIST tradition, by contrast, suggests that reflection and reason provide the surer guide.

3 THE REJECTION OF METAPHYSICS

I have tried to identify what I have called the traditional role of philosophy, according to which the philosopher's main task was to give a metaphysical account of the world. I now want to consider briefly the reasons which lead to a rejection of metaphysics and, consequently, to the search for a new role for philosophy.

The most important factor has been the rise of modern science, and the realisation that its success has been due to the refusal to accept any views about the world which are not supported by evidence. 'Giving an account of the world in the most general terms' has come to seem a better description of science than of philosophy. And the metaphysician has been accused of trying to do, by armchair reflection, what can only be done by the empirical methods of science.

This point of view found extreme expression in a movement called LOGICAL POSITIVISM which originated in Vienna during the nineteen twenties. Metaphysics had been attacked earlier in the century on the grounds that it was idle, in the way in which speculation as to whether there exists life in other galaxies is idle, since there is no way in which the accuracy of such speculation could be checked. Part of the motivation of the earlier positivism, as indeed of the later, came from a concern for science; physicists were themselves concerned about the introduction into physics of 'unobservables', concepts like the atom, on the grounds that physics should confine itself to what was observable. But the logical positivists, or neo-positivists, objected to metaphysical statements on entirely new grounds. Metaphysical statements pose as candidates for knowledge, appearing to say something true or false about the world, when in fact they say nothing; they literally lack sense. The ultimate grounds for denying meaning to metaphysical statements were provided by a principle of verification, according to which the meaning of a statement is the circumstances in which it will be accepted as true. Statements have meaning only in so far as we know, at least in principle, in what circumstances they would be true. They can, therefore, be directly verified (like 'this is red') or can be shown by logical analysis to be reducible to other statements which can be directly verifiable. And metaphysical statements are neither directly verifiable nor reducible to other statements, by logical analysis, which are directly verifiable.

Philosophy, then, can provide us with no knowledge about the world; it has no subject matter. Instead, it is a method – the method of logical analysis of language. As Schlick put it,

Philosophy is that activity through which the meaning of statements is revealed or determined. By means of philosophy statements are explained, by means of science they are verified.

4 RUSSELL'S THEORY OF DESCRIPTIONS; A PARADIGM OF ANALYSIS

The view that philosophy is analysis was not confined to the logical positivists. The developments in logic on which they relied were due mainly to Russell. I won't attempt to trace the exact nature of the debt; it concerned the logical relationship between those statements which, though meaningful, were not directly verifiable, and those statements (called elementary or protocol statements) which were directly verifiable. Instead, I will look briefly at the 'paradigm of analysis' (as another philosopher, F. P. Ramsey, called it) which Russell provided in his theory of descriptions, first formulated in 1905.

Russell was concerned with the problem of how sentences like 'The king of France is bald' could have meaning in the absence of a king of France. The grammatical construction of the sentence suggests that it is about something, i.e. the grammatical subject of the sentence, 'the king of France'; and that something is said about that subject in the rest of the sentence, i.e. in the predicate, 'is bald'. But how can the sentence be about the king of France if there is no such person? The conclusion, which Russell accepted with increasing reluctance, was that though the king of France did not exist in the normal sense (in the sense in which the queen of England exists) nevertheless he must exist in some other sense. If there is no entity named by 'the king of France' in the physical world, nevertheless there must be an entity somewhere (perhaps in a special realm of meaning) for the phrase to name. Otherwise the sentence 'The king of France is bald' would lack meaning, which it obviously doesn't. Implicit in this argument is the assumption that in the final analysis words have meaning only if they are the names of things which actually exist in the world.

Russell's answer was to suggest that the grammatical form of the sentence 'The king of France is bald' (and others like it in containing as apparent subject phrases of the form 'the so and so') was misleading as to its true or logical form. And the analysis of such sentences which he offered in his theory of descriptions claimed to display their true or logical form. The details of the analysis are unimportant in the present connection, but I will mention them for the sake of completeness. 'The king of France is bald' was analysed as the conjunction 'There is a king of France; there is not more than one king of France; and there is nothing which is the king of France and which is not bald.' What is important is the advantage claimed for the analysis; that it enables us to say that the sentence analysed has meaning (though it is false) by displaying the true or logical form of the original sentence. In other words, it reflects more accurately the form of reality, since reality does not contain a non-existent king of France. But views about what reality does and does not contain I have already said are metaphysical. So Russell justified the practice of analysis on metaphysical grounds; originally implicitly so, and later (in his Monist articles on logical atomism) explicitly so.

I have tried, very briefly, to indicate some of the factors which lead to the introduction of analysis into philosophy. Now I want to look at the result of the fact that philosophy came to be identified with analysis, and at the new role for philosophy which emerged.

5 PHILOSOPHY AS DISTINGUISHED BY ITS METHODS

If the philosopher is to practise the method of analysis, he must practise it *on* something. What he practises it on is, of course, language; but which bits of language? Russell and the logical positivists were directed in their activities by their concern with metaphysics; either by the desire to put forward a particular metaphysical view or to reject the possibility of metaphysics altogether. But if the rejection of metaphysics is taken seriously, what then? For the implication of the view which I am considering is that philosophy has no distinctive subject matter, and that there are no genuine philosophic problems.

But even if there are no genuine philosophic problems, many people have in the past supposed that there were. So the analytic philosopher still has a task – that of clearing up the puzzlement created by supposing that problems exist where none in fact exists. The source of such puzzlement, on this view, lies in our language – the language we use to describe the world, rather than in anything intrinsically puzzling in the world itself. The philosopher's task is therapeutic; not solving problems, but showing that what have been taken as problems are not problems after all. Given a better understanding of our language – possibly using the technique of linguistic (or conceptual) analysis – such problems will simply melt away, like the morning mist when the sun comes out.

Time, for example, has always been thought to present a philosophical problem. Few people can have failed to be puzzled, at some time or other, by the question: 'When did time begin?'; since any possible answer seems to lead to the further question: 'What happened before that?' The original question seems a proper one, like: 'When did the Wars of the Roses begin?'; but one which we are prevented from answering, not by ignorance, but because *any* answer like 'AD 1066' or 'AD 1492' is obviously going to be unsatisfactory. It seems like a proper question; it is grammatically well formed (like 'Caesar was a Roman'), but it offends against the rules of logical syntax (like 'Caesar is a prime number'). Just as Russell used logical analysis to do a salvage job on 'the king of France is bald', so, too, logical analysis can be used to show that 'When did time begin?' is beyond salvage.

To do this job properly would involve giving a correct account of the logic of temporal sentences; I won't attempt to stray into this difficult field. But an early fruit of the application of logical analysis gave some indication of the sort of mistake which is involved in asking a question like 'When did time begin?' We are led astray because we try to understand time by thinking of it as like something else which we think we understand already. We rely, that is, on a metaphor. We think perhaps of time as like a river, or as like a bird flying through a room; and of events as something like beads, strung together by an invisible thread. Such metaphors are not entirely misconceived; time passes relentlessly, just as the waters of the river flow on unceasingly to the sea. But metaphors can lead us astray if we do not realise their limitations: if they lead us to ask, for example, 'How fast does the river of time flow?', since we can certainly ask of geographical rivers how fast they flow; and 'Where (or when) did it begin?', since, again, all geographical rivers begin somewhere.

All this may seem far removed from education. In a later chapter I hope to show that it isn't, by examining in some detail the metaphor involved in talk of the aims of education.

6 PHILOSOPHY AS A SECOND-ORDER ACTIVITY

The philosopher, therefore, may find employment in dealing with those problems traditionally regarded as philosophic by showing that we have been mistaken in regarding them as problems. Philosophy would continue to exist, but only by devouring its capital of past error; it has nothing positive to contribute. But, even if this is correct, it might still eke out a living, putting its own special methods and techniques to new uses, by taking in other people's problems. This is the view, which commands considerable acceptance today, of philosophy as a second-order activity.

Before attempting to say what is meant by a second-order activity, I ought to say what a first-order activity is. I have already distinguished in chapter one between practical activities like education, and theoretical activities like physics, psychology and sociology. But, from the present point of view, what is important is that both sorts of activity involve the use of language. Those engaged in practical activities will have to make decisions as to what to do. Such decisions are often expressed in words and defended or criticised by the use of other words. Often, and especially when anything like democratic procedures are followed, such decisions are preceded by discussion. And those engaged in theoretical disciplines express their results in language; they use language to communicate the knowledge they have gained to others – to others in the same field in order to gain the publicity necessary to science and to those to whom the knowledge may be of use or interest. The language typical of the discussion in-involved in a particular activity may be referred to as the DIS-COURSE of that activity; so one might speak of the language of science as scientific discourse, of the language of education as educational discourse. Of course, in one sense the scientist and the educationalist may use the same language, say English; while two scientists may use different languages, say English and French.

What distinguishes one discourse from another is not the natural language used, but the concepts which are typical of it. Of course, we can only refer to these by using words, but it is the idea, rather than the actual words used to express it, which is important.

Philosophy as a second-order discipline, then, concerns itself, not with the subject-matter of first-order disciplines, but with the medium in which they are conducted; that is, with the discourse peculiar to them and the procedures implicit in them. Very roughly, the philosopher stands in the same sort of relationship to the participant in a first order activity as the mechanic stands to the operator of a machine. The philosopher is like the 'trouble shooter' – the man who locates a fault in a computer, a fault revealed by the faulty operation of the computer. But the philosopher is not concerned with machines, but with language; or rather with the clarification of concepts, especially with the black sheep, the ones that give trouble. Examples would be 'motivation', 'emotion' and 'thought' in psychology; 'purpose' in biology; 'society' in sociology; and, of course, 'education', 'knowledge', 'learning' and 'teaching' in education. What is really needed, of course, is examples of philosophical explication of such concepts; I will try to provide this for the central educational concepts in succeeding chapters. But it is worth noting in passing that there are certain very general concepts which seem to pervade all our thinking – like 'space' and 'time', 'things' (or 'material objects'), 'facts' and 'truth', and that these are just the ones which have always attracted the attention of philosophers.

First-order activities not only ask questions, but also offer answers to them. This is so whether the activity is theoretical, in which case the answer states that something is the case, or whether it is practical, in which case the answer states that something should be done. And in both cases the answers provided are claimed to be correct. But if this is so there must be some way in which correct and incorrect answers can be distinguished from each other. These means may be referred to as CRITERIA OF VALIDITY. Such criteria are often taken for granted. The philosopher is therefore concerned, firstly, to make them explicit and, once this is done, to assess them to see whether they really do the job which is claimed for them.

At first sight the claim made for philosophy as a second-order activity seems modest enough. Philosophy achieves a positive role, but only by applying its methods to a borrowed subject matter. The difficulty is, however, that you can't borrow someone else's subject matter as you might borrow their car or flat for the weekend. Criticism of the language of science or psychology is likely to be misconceived unless it is based on the sort of familiarity with science or psychology possessed by the scientist or psychologist himself. Fortunately, this difficulty is not so great in the case of practical activities like education, politics and morality. Most people, at some time or other, and to a greater or lesser degree, have some experience of these as participants. Morality, for example, is a pervasive feature of all our lives (or at least of those of us who are not psychotic); though some moral philosophers, it must be admitted, write as though they had never met a genuine moral problem in their lives. (It is for this reason that Sartre has acquired a reputation as a moral philosopher; he at least demonstrates convincingly that he does know what a moral problem looks like.) On the other hand, it is much less clear that practical activities possess criteria of validity of their own. This is an important problem in ETHICS (the second-order consideration of morality). In discussing the difference between an arbitrary and a rational solution to an educational problem I suggested that the relevance of a reason to a problem required not only factual knowledge of the context but also a realisation of the point of activity. It is for this reason that, just as the question 'what is morality' is important for ethics (though an answer to it is presupposed in moral practice itself), so too the question 'what is education' is important in the philosophy of education (though, again, an answer to it is implicit in any discussion of educational problems).

7   THE POSSIBILITY OF AN INDEPENDENT ROLE FOR PHILOSOPHY: PHILOSOPHY AS A SUPER-SCIENCE

The point of engaging in philosophy as a second-order activity is that by doing so a contribution is made, though indirectly, to the solution of the problems of the relevant first-order activity. If there is ambiguity about what those problems are, there will also be confusion about what would *count* as a solution to them. A proposal for an educational change cannot be put into practice if it is confused, ambiguous or self-contradictory, since nothing would count as putting it into practice.

I want now to consider the possibility of a more independent role for philosophy. I will consider two suggestions about the way in which this might come about; the first, that philosophy is a sort of super-science, I want to reject; towards the second I am much more sympathetic.

Particular forms of knowledge, provided by the various theoretical disciplines such as physics, chemistry, biology, psychology and so on, provide only partial accounts of the world; they are selective in their approach. Might not the philosopher combine the knowledge gained from such particular sources into one synoptic view of the world? adding, perhaps, the results of religious experience and the insights of literature, history and art as a sort of flavouring, like herbs in a stew. I think the logical positivists were inclined to such a view, though they would certainly have omitted the flavouring; at any rate, their rejection of metaphysics was not intended to exclude such a possibility. And one way of achieving such a synthesis would be of showing that the various discourses by which one discipline is separated from another are not different after all. The logical positivists certainly thought that this could be done; one of their principal aims was to provide a 'unified language of natural science'. On the face of it, it does seem as though psychological statements (statements about beliefs, thoughts, emotions and so on) are different from the statements of physical science (which are about physical bodies and their movements and interaction). So part of the programme of creating the unified language of science consists of showing that such differences are only apparent and that statements about minds can be shown to be equivalent in meaning to statements about physical bodies and their movements. My objections to such attempts are twofold; firstly, no one has yet shown that such a programme can be carried out (though it would be rash to say either that anyone had shown that it could *not* be carried out); and, secondly, the motive for such an attempt is a metaphysical one which I see no reason to share, i.e. the belief that only the entities with which physics deals are ultimately real.

I do think that the findings of particular theoretical disciplines need to be brought together if they are to have application in practical activities. But I have already indicated that I think they are brought together by the problems of those activities; there is no separate activity of synthesis. What unity the theoretical disciplines share apart from this springs from their roots in the common experience we all share, and from which they spring.

8 THE POSSIBILITY OF AN INDEPENDENT ROLE FOR PHILOSOPHY: THE INDEPENDENCE OF EPISTEMOLOGY

Philosophy appeared to lose its independent role when what I called the traditional view of philosophy was replaced by the view of philosophy as analysis. But perhaps these two views are not so opposed as they seem to be. G. E. Moore was one of the principal figures in the development of modern analytic philosophy. Nevertheless he made the following remark in chapter one of *Some Main Problems of Philosophy*:

The most important and interesting thing that philosophers have tried to do is . . . to give a general description of the whole of the Universe, mentioning all the more important kinds of things which we know to be in it . . .' and the way 'they are related to one another'.

But Moore himself did not attempt to provide an account of this sort. Instead, he asked:

1. How does Common Sense answer this question?

2. In what ways do particular philosophic views add to or take away from this Common Sense view?

Further, it turns out that the Common Sense view is not to be established empirically by asking ordinary men of common sense, but by reference to our ordinary ways of talking and the analysis of what we ordinarily say; that is, by an examination of language.

How does this open up the possibility of a reconciliation between the traditional view of philosophy as providing a metaphysical view of the world and the view of philosophy as distinguished by its analytic methods? Anyone who wishes to put forward a metaphysical thesis about what is really the case, in contrast to what appears to be the case, must nevertheless provide an account of how things appear, if only to make clear what is being denied. Bradley, for example, who contrasts Appearance and Reality, nevertheless thought that Reality could be approached only by way of appearance. And McTaggart preceded his denial of the reality of time by an account of time as it 'appears to us *prima facie*'. They went on, of course, to deny that the way things appear to us provides us with an accurate account of reality; their ground for doing so was that their description of the appearance of things did not present us with an account of a possible world, since it involved logical contradictions. Of course, they could have, more modestly, concluded that their account of how things appear was mistaken, instead of supposing that they were turning a dialectical key in the door of Reality.

I do not wish to suggest that nothing could lead us to revise our conception of how things are, but merely to emphasise that any departure from the Common Sense point of view requires justification. How things appear to be must be the starting point of any such revision, if only because there could be no other starting point. We normally suppose, for example, that the world contains physical objects like chairs; and anyone who wishes to deny this must bear the burden of proof. Similarly, anyone who wishes to deny that the world does not contain minds as well as bodies – a denial implicit in the programme of providing a 'unified language of natural science', to which I referred earlier – has to provide positive grounds for his denial.

But how do things appear to us? In general, what is it to have a conception of reality? In the case of education, what do those engaged in the activity take themselves to be doing? These are questions which can only be answered by way of a consideration of the language which we use to describe the world and in which we speak of our activities in education. Both the possibilities of belief and experience, and the possibilities of action open to us, are limited by the concepts which we have.

All this will be elaborated later. For the moment I think I have said as much as I can usefully say in answer to the question, 'what is philosophy?'

SUMMARY

1. Twentieth-century philosophy is, for good reasons, very much preoccupied with questions of language. The chapter tries to explain how this came about.

2. In the past, philosophers have been primarily concerned to give a metaphysical account of the world. Epistemology (theory of knowledge) has also been important, though it has tended to be regarded as of secondary importance.

3. The logical positivists rejected metaphysics on the grounds that its statements lacked sense, since they are unverifiable in principle and not merely in practice (i.e. nothing would count for or against their truth). Philosophy is, instead, the activity of providing a logical analysis of language.

4. Russell had already provided a 'paradigm of analysis' in his theory of descriptions, although his philosophical motivation was different.

5. Even if philosophy has no genuine problems of its own, the method of analysis can find employment showing that what have been traditionally regarded as the problems of philosophy are not genuine problems at all.

6. Philosophy also finds employment as a second-order activity, examining the discourse of first-order practical activities like morality, religion or education, and theoretical activities like physics and psychology. The criteria of validity implicit in the various first-order activities are also examined.

7. A possible role claimed for philosophy has been that of a super-science.

8. Whether or not philosophy is able to provide an account of the reality which lies behind the appearances of things, it may still have a role to play in offering an account of how things appear to us. But an account of our conception of reality can only be given by way of an analysis of the language in which that conception is expressed. Similarly,

an account may be offered of what those engaged in the activity of education take themselves to be doing by way of an analysis of the language of education.

FURTHER READING

1. For an outline of the changes which have occurred in philosophy in the twentieth century, see Ayer (11) and Warnock (103). Passmore (65) provides a broader and more detailed account of the last hundred years, giving also many detailed references. Urmson (98) is clear, but more specialised and therefore more technical. See also the later chapters of O'Connor (60). For an introduction to philosophical analysis, see Hospers (48).

2. On metaphysics, see Pears (68) and Walsh (102). On epistemology, see references in chapter 7.

3. The most important English statement of the logical positivist point of view is by Ayer (8). Ayer (9) is a collection of articles by some of the main members of the original Vienna Circle; see also his own introduction to that volume. For Schlick see Ayer (9, page 56).

4. Russell's original 1905 article is reprinted in Marsh (53); the Monist articles on logical atomism are also reprinted in the same volume.

5. For examples of the new logical analysis at work, see the collections of articles edited by Flew (31, 32, and 33) and also Flew's own introductions. On 'time' see Findlay (in 32) and Smart (in 31).

6. Ethics is, for Hare (41), the logical study of the language of morals. For the practical importance of language, see Stevenson (93, especially chapter 3) and Scheffler (87, especially on 'pragmatic' definitions, pages 19 to 22). See also Corbett's contribution to Archambault (4). For examples of the second-order approach to psychology, see Hamlyn (39) and Peters (70).

7. Liberal studies are generally held to be desirable, but there seems to be a great deal of confusion about why; for clarification, see Hirst (115, chapter 5). Scheffler (87, especially chapters 1 and 3) discusses confusions which arise due to uncritical acceptance of definitions, slogans, and metaphors in education. (He also discusses the view of philosophy as a super-science.)

On the reformulation of the sentences of psychology in physical language see Carnap (chapter 8 in 9). For a recent version of the same theme, see Smart (92).

8. Winch (106, especially chapter 1) expresses, better than I have been able to do, the view of philosophy with which I am most sympathetic. On Moore's views, see Moore (56, especially chapters 2 and 7).

3 Language and Meaning

In a later chapter (chapter 5) I propose to offer an account of 'education', according to which to become educated is to learn to be a person; adding that the most important part of learning to be a person is acquiring a conception of reality. I wish, however, to avoid identifying the having of concepts with the possession of the language used to express them, though, of course, the acquisition of new and more sophisticated concepts is facilitated, and to a great extent made possible, by the possession of language. So before going on to talk about language I want to distinguish words and concepts.

Concepts are connected with seeing the world as displaying order. To have the concept of redness is to see red things as displaying a distinguishable aspect of reality. Language, on the other hand, is connected with communication. To know the meaning of the word 'red' is to be in a position to say to someone else that an aspect of reality displays the quality of redness. To say something is to say something which can be understood by someone else. Language is essentially a public, social phenomenon. It allows the possibility of a shared conception of the world, of seeing the world as ordered in the same way as others see it as ordered. The conception of the world open to non-language-users is essentially SOLIPSISTIC; that is, purely personal and idiosyncratic. Crusoe on his desert island, even if he had been alone there since birth, would, of course, have seen things as ordered. He would have noted for himself the alternation of day and night, picked out the trees which bore edible fruit and experienced the difference between the hardness of bare rock and the softness of grass or sand. But he could share his conception of his

c

island with no one, since there was no-one there with whom to
share it. And it is unlikely that the native-born Crusoe I have
imagined would have come to see his island quite as it would
have appeared to the shipwrecked mariner of the story. The order
we see in the world depends on the concepts we impose on it;
though, of course, we are not free to impose any concepts on the
world. A native-born and a shipwrecked Crusoe would share a
common sensory equipment and have the same basic needs for
food, water and shelter; and, living on the same island, it would
be surprising if they did not make many distinctions in common.
But the Crusoe from civilisation would bring with him many
concepts which had application on the island, but which it had
never occurred to the native-born Crusoe to make; fine colour
distinctions, for example, which had no practical importance on
the island, while the latter would see differences which were not
apparent to the newcomer. Common-language-users, on the
other hand, do to a very much greater extent share the same conception of the world; nor is this surprising, since a large part of
that conception has been acquired socially, with the help of
language.

Concepts cannot, in any case, be identified with the language
we use to express them. Before the word 'red' can be linked with
the redness of a particular object, not only must redness be picked
out as a recurrent feature of the landscape, but so also must the
sound made when the word 'red' is spoken. Language can only
be acquired, therefore, by those whose world is already to some
extent ordered or conceptualised. The young child must acquire a
primitive conception of the world as ordered, which has something in common with that of an adult, before it could begin to
acquire language; though even that part of its conception of the
world presumably becomes modified with the acquisition of
language.

I shall have more to say about having a conception of the world
in chapter 5 (page 60). In the rest of this chapter I propose to
leave concepts on one side, and to look instead at the sort of
philosophical problem language has been thought to offer.

2 THE PROBLEM OF MEANING

We do succeed in communicating with one another by means of language; the philosophical problem is how language can be related to the world in such a way as to make this possible. It is not very obvious that there is a problem here; the explicit recognition of it is a comparatively recent development in philosophy. This is not to say that the adoption of a theory of meaning by a philosopher is anything new, but the tendency has been to accept such theories uncritically and implicitly. I think Russell's problem about sentences like 'The king of France is bald' (chapter two, page 22) was in part generated by a theory of meaning which, at least initially, was held uncritically.

What is the problem of meaning? In language (or any form of symbolism, such as pictorial road signs, shop signs like the barber's pole, or pictures by the pegs in the infants' cloakroom) one thing stands for another: the word 'red' stands for the quality of redness; the name 'Fido' stands for the dog Fido. But how is the symbol related to that which it symbolises?

The problem is how, in general, language has meaning; how language is possible. If we assume a context in which language is already used (if we assume also, therefore, that language is possible), there is no special difficulty about saying how new expressions are introduced into the language. Many expressions acquire meaning by means of verbal definitions. A heifer, according to the *Concise Oxford Dictionary*, is a young cow that has not had calf. Such a definition tells us that the word 'heifer' means the same as (or is synonymous with) the expression 'young cow that has not had calf'. Provided, therefore, the latter expression has a meaning with which we are already acquainted, the definition informs us of the meaning of the word being defined, or lays down a meaning for it if the word is being introduced into the language for the first time. But this account can't be generalised and offered as an account of how language in general acquires meaning, since that problem is the problem of how it is possible for language to reach out to something beyond itself. How, for example, can the sentence 'Tiggy and Gertrude are just good friends' be related to two people and the relationship between them? Or the sentence 'The Emperor of China sleeps in a gold-painted bed', be related to the Emperor of China and his sleeping habits? The sentences as I have written them consist of marks on paper in my typewriter; how can the marks on the paper be related to two characters drinking together in the public bar of the *Pig and Whistle*? Or to a dignified, portly gentleman in silk pyjamas six thousand miles away? They are related because the ink marks on the paper are not merely ink marks, but have meaning or significance. But this is just to restate the problem; how is the symbol related to that which it symbolises? To offer an answer to this question is to put forward a theory of meaning.

One such theory is to regard all words as the names of things. Professor Ryle has called this the 'FIDO'—FIDO THEORY, since it starts by supposing that there is no problem about how the word 'Fido' is related to the dog of that name, and goes on to suggest that all words get their meaning in a similar way. But even if all sentences can be shown to consist only of names in arrangement, there remains the problem of how names acquire meaning. All language, on this view, is regarded as ultimately dependent for its meaning on those parts of language which are closest to the world; where the gap between language and the world is at its narrowest. But unless one is prepared to accept the relationship between a name and what it names as obvious and requiring no explanation, nothing is gained unless an account of how names themselves acquire meaning is given. To talk of an act of pointing (OSTENSION) is not much help, since pointing is itself a symbolic activity. Nor does it help to invoke a mental act of meaning, since what I *meant* to say (i.e. intended to say) is normally contrasted with what I did say (i.e. with the meaning of what I said).

The present trend of philosophical opinion is to reject any suggestion that there is any part of language which is privileged so far as the having of meaning is concerned. The tendency is therefore to abandon the search for meaning altogether, or to admit that no simple, precise account of meaning is possible. Instead, language is related to more general human activity; it is an integral part of that activity and cannot be understood in isolation from it. And, as human activity is rich and varied, so too is the language which is a part of it. All words are not names, and describing things is not the only use to which language is put. This point of view is sometimes summed up by the slogan: 'Don't ask for the meaning, ask for the use.' What this amounts to is: 'Don't ask for *the* way language is related to the world (or don't ask for *the* meaning); ask for the *ways* in which language is related to the world.' And now the world is seen as containing not just 'facts' or 'objects', but people *doing* things.

What follows from this point of view is that language can only be acquired if there is the opportunity of seeing how others use words; of learning not just how words can properly be joined together to form sentences, but coming to understand the circumstances in which such sentences can be used to say something. Hence the importance of a culturally, and particularly linguistically, rich environment for young children. This is a necessary condition of learning to talk, though it is not a sufficient condition. Babies learn to talk, household pets do not. How children learn to talk is a mystery, but it is a psychological mystery to which psychologists may one day provide an answer. The philosophical problem is to try to make clear what talking (or saying something) is.

3 MEANING AND TRUTH

Whatever account is given of meaning, it is important to distinguish between meaning and truth. Purported sentences divide into those which lack meaning (and are, therefore, not really sentences at all) and those which possess meaning. The logical positivists, for example, claimed that the statements of metaphysics lacked meaning. Carnap quoted a passage from Heidegger which ends with the sentence: 'The Nothing itself nothings'; his own example was 'Caesar is a prime number'. Lacking meaning, such sentences cannot be used to make any statement which is either true or false, since nothing would count for or against their truth or falsity.

Sentences which possess meaning, on the other hand, can be used to make statements which may be either true or false. Linguistic expressions are not custom-built to fit actual situations, but possible situations. Language is necessarily flexible; as Russell puts it: 'you can understand a proposition when you understand the words of which it is composed even though you never heard the proposition before.' So the sentence 'Tiggy and Gertrude are just good friends' has meaning, and can be understood even by someone who does not know whether it is true or false. Anyone who uses it to make a statement will normally be taken to be putting it forward as a true statement, but the statement he makes may be false, through either error or insincerity.

So 'The cat is on the mat' has meaning if, roughly speaking, we have given a meaning to the words and if the arrangement of the words is syntactically correct. If we know what 'The cat is on the mat' means we know what it would be like for the cat to be on the mat. And the cat can be truthfully said to be on the mat if the cat is in fact on the mat. I don't wish to suggest that 'truth' presents any fewer difficulties to the philosopher than 'meaning', but whatever account is given of them the distinction between meaning and truth must be maintained.

4 THE CONVENTIONAL NATURE OF SYMBOLISM

I suggested earlier that the possession of concepts was not confined to language-users; for example, rats can be trained to discriminate between doors labelled with either a triangle or a circle. One door may lead to water, and the other to food; the rats can learn to choose the correct door acording to whether they are hungry or thirsty. And it seems natural to compare this situation with that of the cook in the kitchen faced with a row of ceramic jars labelled 'basil', 'marjoram' and 'rosemary'. The cook knows that the label 'basil' means that the jar contains basil; in the same way should we not say that the rat knows that the label on the door leading to food means that the door leads to food?

I think, however, that the behaviour of the rats can be adequately described in terms which do not involve this conclusion. In order to distinguish between the two situations, therefore, I propose to make a distinction between symbols and signs. The meaning I attach to these terms may not be an accurate description of the way they are normally used; if so, I may be taken to be offering stipulative definitions of them. Symbols are used with the intention of communicating information to others (or perhaps recording it for the user's own convenience). The labels on the jars are symbols; and they would still be symbols even if they did not take the form of words but pictures of the herbs themselves; just as a triangle or a circle on the door of an East European public lavatory is a symbol and not a sign. The labels were put on the jars in order to inform the cook of their contents. They were put there on the confident and quite justified assumption that they would be seen for what they are; that their purpose would be realised and their meaning understood by the cook. The cook need not even know what marjoram looks like; indeed, she could find out what it looks like by looking in the jar labelled 'marjoram'.

The rat situation looks similar because the door leading to food was marked differently from the door leading to water by the person conducting the experiment, and this was done in order to provide a basis on which the rat could learn to discriminate between the door leading to food and the door leading to water. And rats can learn to make discriminations of this sort. But while the experimenter, if shrunk to fit the test apparatus and suitably deprived of food or water, would soon come to see the triangle and the circle as symbols, just as the cook sees the labels on the herb jars as symbols, it does not follow that they appear as symbols to the rat. For rats do not themselves use symbols; they do not make noises, or make marks on paper or doors, in order to inform anybody of anything. They learn to discriminate between the two doors on the basis of the circle and the triangle because things have been arranged so that they provide the only available basis of discrimination. There are no grounds at all for saying that the rats are aware that the doors have been marked as they have been in order to tell them whether they lead to food or water. Accordingly I shall say that the triangle and the circle function as *signs* of food or water for the rat, but they do not *symbolise* food or water for it.

It follows from the way I have distinguished between symbols and signs that the relationship between symbol and symbolised will be different from that between sign and significate. The connection between symbol and symbolised is provided by a meaning rule which is established conventionally. Meaning rules are set up by common agreement in practice. The choice of symbol is dictated by convenience; there need be no natural connection between the symbol and that which it symbolises. In other words, meaning is not a property of the symbol itself, as redness is a property of a red ball; nor is the connection between symbol and symbolised something which has always existed and which was discovered by man, like the causal discoveries of science, as language developed. Meaning is given to symbols by the use to which they are put; the choice of a particular symbol for a particular use is dictated only by convenience. This, of course, applies only to the establishment of the meaning rule; once the rule is set up successful communication depends on its observance. We use the word 'red', for example, to refer to the colour red; but we could equally well use a different word, say 'blue', to refer to the same colour. But given the existing rule whereby 'red' is used to refer to red objects, anybody who decides to use the word 'blue' to refer to red objects is unlikely to be understood. (Though they may be, like a child who always refers to a fork as a 'knife'; if it asks for a knife, it will get what it wants if it is handed a fork.)

The connection between a sign and what it is a sign of is normally a natural one; it is not set up by human intervention. The standard example is the lightning which is a sign of thunder to come. That the lightning is a sign of the thunder is the result of a natural connection between thunder and lightning; it is not open to anyone to change the sign of thunder from lightning to three blasts on a quarry siren, to avoid the inconvenience of blasted oaks or stricken church steeples. No one uses the lightning to warn anyone of anything; it is just a natural fact that the lightning can be expected to be followed by thunder. If this expectation were hardly ever fulfilled, the lightning could not be said to be a sign of thunder; whereas the label 'marjoram' on the herb jar would retain its symbolic status even if the jar never contained anything but hair pins.

There are many examples of signs actually produced by one animal which function as signals to others. The warning cry of a blackbird, for example, is a direct response to certain specific stimuli (which can be identified using the experimental techniques developed by ethologists) rather than to anything which could properly be described as the presence of danger; and the young respond directly to the cry by crouching low in the nest. But it would be wrong to say that the blackbird makes the cry in order to warn the nestlings, and that they understand the warning and act in the light of their understanding. The main difference between this situation and that of the rats is probably in the amount of learning involved; the rats could only have learnt the connection between the signs on the doors and what they signified.

In later sections I shall be concerned with symbolism, especially in its most sophisticated form of spoken and written language (though, as I have defined 'symbol', pictorial inn signs and road signs are symbols and not signs).

5 SPOKEN AND WRITTEN LANGUAGE

It is a CONTINGENT fact about human beings (i.e. a fact which might have been otherwise) that they are capable of producing, almost from birth, a very great variety of sounds through the use of their vocal chords. It is to this fact, presumably, that spoken language owes its primacy and that children learn to speak before they learn to write. Spoken language is very convenient for many purposes; for buying groceries, for example, or chatting up dollies. But sometimes it is convenient to order by post, or possible only to express one's love by letter. Written communications are more time-consuming, and writing material is not always ready to hand, but they have advantages in producing a permanent record and in not requiring the physical presence of the second party. So of course reading and writing are basic skills in modern society. But the difference between the sound which is made when the word 'red' is spoken, and the shape on paper when it is written, are incidental to its role as a symbol. What is important to it as a symbol is that it is used to refer to a particular colour, and this, its meaning, is the same whether the word is spoken or written. So, though reading and writing are important in the early schooling of the child, and are rightly emphasised both as keys to future learning and essential to social competence, the difference between spoken and written language is one of comparative detail. In the same way, reading can be thought of as the visual perception of language, compared with the aural perception of it in its spoken form. But what is said when 'The cat is on the mat' is spoken or written, and what is understood when it is heard or read, is the same; just as it is the same statement which is made whether it is spoken in French or in English.

Books used to teach children to read almost always contain both written material and pictures. On the view which I have presented here, the picture of the cat sitting on the mat is just as much a symbolic representation as the caption underneath it reading 'The cat is on the mat'. Why, then, does the presence of the picture help the child to understand what the sentence says?

It would be a difficult though not a hopeless task to teach a child to understand the symbolism in written form if it did not already understand it in spoken form. (It would not be impossible; children who are completely deaf and dumb can learn to read.) But normally the meaning of what is said in the written sentence is not new to the child; what is new is the form of symbolism used. In learning to read it is mastering a new form of symbolism, not learning new language; though, of course, once it can read its linguistic competence can then be enlarged through reading. And though the picture of the cat on the mat is a written form of symbolism, like the sentence underneath it, it is a form of symbolism which is easily mastered by the child; so easily so, in fact, that it is tempting to suppose that no use of symbolism is involved – or at least, that in this case the connection between the symbol and the symbolised is a natural one and not dependent on convention. That the drawing of the cat stands for a cat, for example, seems to depend on some intrinsic feature of the drawing of the cat, such as its shape, rather than on a conventional meaning rule. And if the same thing goes for the mat, then the natural way to interpret the picture is to suppose that the relationship between the actual cat and the actual mat is mirrored in the relationship between the part of the picture representing the cat and the part of the picture representing the mat.

What is probably correct here is that the picture is a symbolic representation, but that there are similarities (which are obvious even to a young child) between the symbol and what it symbolises which make it easy to see what the symbol is intended to be a symbol of. Drawing the cat in red, for example, is an obvious way to indicate that it is a red cat which is being symbolised. But that the actual colour of the drawing of the cat shows the colour of the actual cat is a convention which could be different. The convention could be that blue in the picture meant that the cat was red. Certainly the king's crown is more often yellow than gold; though one takes it that a gold crown is meant. To use blue in the picture to mean red would be confusing – only a government department would adopt such a convention – but it is just as possible as a convention as using red to indicate red.

The advantage of using symbols which bear a similarity to that which they symbolise is that this provides an obvious mnemonic as to their meaning; it does not mean that they do not have a meaning; or that a different meaning could not have been attached to the same symbols. The symbolism of ordinary written language forgoes any such advantage; no one is inclined to see any obvious resemblance between the written word 'cat' and shape of actual cats any more than there is a resemblance between the sound made when the word 'cat' is spoken and the caterwauling of cats. But ordinary verbal language, in relying solely on conventional meaning rules, frees itself from any restrictions on what can be said imposed by the intrinsic nature of the symbol; much more can be said, more precisely, by means of words than by means of pictures.

SUMMARY

1. Concepts cannot be identified with the words used to express them; though the possession of language facilitates the acquisition of new concepts and makes possible the acquisition of more sophisticated concepts.

2. The philosophic problem of meaning is the problem of how language is possible; of how language, in general, is related to the

world. There is no *one* way in which language is related to the world; words are not all names of things, for example. Rather, language is used for a variety of purposes, and is an integral part of a variety of human activities.

3. Not everything which looks like a sentence possesses meaning. Sentences which possess meaning can be used to make statements which are either true or false; such statements are normally put forward as true by the person making them.

4. A distinction was made between symbols which are used to communicate and natural signs. Symbols are given a meaning by conventional meaning rules. Signs do not have meaning in this sense; they have merely been found to provide a reliable indication of the presence, or impending presence, of something else.

5. The symbolism used in language may take the form of sounds (i.e. spoken language), or marks on paper (written language); but the meaning of a word is the same whether the word is spoken or written. Children normally learn to talk before they learn to write, and to understand what is said to them before they learn to read. The symbolism of pictures is easier to understand than that of the written word, and pictures in reading books provide the child with a clue as to the meaning of the captions under them.

FURTHER READING

1. On concepts, see references for chapter 5, section 3 (page 72). On the view I have presented, it is possible to possess concepts which are shared with no one else, though most of our concepts we do as a matter of fact share with others; whereas language is necessarily social. The literature on 'private languages' is relevant here: see Wittgenstein (107, Part One, sections 243 to 315) and Ayer (7, chapter 2).

On the different conceptions of the island of the native-born and the shipwrecked Crusoe, see Waismann (in 32, chapter 7, especially section 3). In the text I have overlooked the possibility of a shared conception of the world based on social behaviour of non-language-users such as chimpanzees or porpoises (if, that is, they are non-language users).

2. On the theory of meaning, and especially the 'Fido' Fido theory, see Ryle (chapter 9 in 18). For a detailed and careful presentation of the view that all meaningful sentences consist of names in arrangement see Wittgenstein (108). For the view of language as an integral part of a range of social activities, see Wittgenstein's revised views (107). Wittgenstein makes difficult reading; for help with the interpretation

of the *Tractatus*, see Black (17); on both the *Tractatus* and the *Investigations* see Pitcher (74). On the philosophy of language generally, see Alston (3).

3. For Carnap's views on metaphysical statements, see chapter 3 in Ayer (9). The quotation from Russell is from the second of the lectures on 'The Philosophy of Logical Atomism' (page 193, in Marsh, 53). On 'truth' see references for chapter five, section five (page 73).

4. On symbols see Bradley (22, Book One, chapter one, sections 1 to 12) cf. Morris (58), Osgood (63, chapter 16) and Skinner (90). On the importance of sign-stimuli in animal behaviour, see Tinbergen (96). Hart (43, page 87) contrasts signs and signals.

4 The Aims of Education

I PHILOSOPHERS DOWN-GRADED

The belief that the philosopher is specially equipped, by superior wisdom, to tell others how to conduct themselves is one which goes naturally with what I have called the traditional view of philosophy. The classic example to look at in connection with education is Plato's *Republic*. In the ideal state of the Republic, the philosopher is king, since he is the one who has wisdom, who really knows how things are and who is not taken in by appearance. He has knowledge of the forms of things, not merely opinion gained by acquaintance with the imperfect copies of the forms of things in the sensible world. In the light of this knowledge he is able to say what form the state and society should take, since he is acquainted with the Form of the state, or the Ideal state. He is able to guide practical conduct, since he knows what to aim at; actual states should conform as closely as possible to the Form of the state. And he is able to lay down the objectives and content of education in such a state; the aim of education should be to train those who will be his successors.

Philosophers are nowadays inclined to be more modest in their claims, and I intend to offer no detailed proposals as to what the aims of education should be. But requests for clarification of the aims of education are perennial, and I want to consider, in general terms, what might be involved in such a request. Such requests spring from the feeling, which I share, that discussion of particular educational problems will be more profitably undertaken in the context of an understanding of education as a whole. What is really required is an understanding of the concept of education, and of the related concepts which occur in educational discussion ('teaching', 'learning', 'knowledge', 'punishment', etc.), and the provision of such understanding is a proper philosophical concern.

One way in which this request for an understanding of education as a whole has been met is by the provision of metaphors, rather than by an explicit analysis of the concept of education. Rousseau, for example, comments that man, 'not content to leave everything as nature has made it . . . must needs shape man himself to his notions, as he does the trees in his garden'. But metaphors, though they may help us achieve understanding, may also mislead. I would like, therefore, firstly to make some general remarks on the use of metaphors, and then to look more closely at the metaphor involved in talk of the aims of education.

2 METAPHORS

Metaphors differ from models in the literal sense in that they are verbal, whereas models are physical things. But they fulfil a similar function, and I will consider models first.

What is the relationship between a physical model of an airliner and the airliner of which it is a model? Certainly they will be alike in some respects, though not in all, since, if the supposed model were identical with the airliner itself, it would not be a model, but a replica – number two off the production line, so to speak. The model, for example, may be of the same shape and proportions as the airliner, though made of different material and on a different scale. So the reaction of the model in a wind tunnel may provide a guide to the reaction of the actual airliner to the flow of air over it in flight. The fact that the model differs from what it is a model of – that it is made of wood and not metal, or is painted red and not green – may not matter if the point of the model is to provide information about the importance of shape; though it will mislead if the resistance of wood to air is different from that of metal. On the other hand, colour and markings will be important if the model is to be used to show prospective customers the sort of plane the airway flies.

Metaphors function in a similar way; they suggest that there is an analogy between two things, without actually saying what it is. They are useful in drawing attention to certain features of what we wish to understand by implying an analogy with something we already understand or suppose we understand. But they can also lead us astray; this is what happens when we think of time as like a river, and are then led to ask the sort of questions about time which we could properly ask about rivers. For suggested analogies are never quite complete, just as the model is never quite the same as the thing it is a model of; and if we take them too seriously they may distort our view of the subject of our real interest, or lead us to overlook altogether a whole aspect of that subject which is not reflected in the model. People tend to let metaphors run away with them, especially when they are not fully aware of the fact that they are relying on a metaphor. And, even though the person using a metaphor may be clear about the point he wishes to make, others may misunderstand. Plato's allegory of the cave provides a classic example; that it is richly suggestive is beyond doubt – unfortunately (at least so far as finding out what Plato meant by it) it suggests different things to different people. Consequently it has been a rich source of scholarly dispute.

3 TRAVEL TALK

It is common to speak in education of the aims of education, and of the importance of knowing what you are aiming at. But it is not particularly obvious that 'knowing what you are aiming at' is a metaphor; just as 'knowing where you are going' would be. It is more obvious that the latter would involve the use of a metaphor and I will consider first the sort of point which might be made by the use of it.

Someone who sets out on a journey normally knows both where he is going and how to get there. But, at a pinch, he could probably get by with only one of these. Detailed instructions on how to get there will, if sufficiently precise, enable him to complete his journey successfully, even though he doesn't know where 'there' is when he starts; e.g. 'take ten paces from the three lone pines in the direction of Big Bear Rock and start digging'. Often, however, detailed instructions are out of the question – when, for example, no one has ever been there before, like the South Pole or the moon; and, in any case, for detailed instructions on how to get there to be possible, *someone* must know where 'there' is. Most important, knowledge of the destination is superior to detailed instructions (if there has to be a choice between the two) in that it leaves a reasonably knowledgeable and intelligent person free to vary the route to his destination in the light of changing circumstances encountered on the route.

The metaphor of a journey has not been used extensively in educational discussion; though it was used by Plato in the *Republic* in the Parable of the Ship, in which the special knowledge of the captain, who knows where the ship is going, is compared with the knowledge of the philosopher king. But it might be used to draw attention to the difficulties and drawbacks of basing a course in teacher-training on the rules of thumb acquired by teachers of long experience. It just isn't possible to anticipate in advance every difficulty which might crop up in a classroom and provide instructions on how to deal with it. What is needed is not precise instructions on how to get 'there' (especially when provided by people who have no clear idea where 'there' is themselves), but a clear idea where 'there' is. So, one might say, it is important to know where you are going, in teaching as in the 'journey of life'. But whatever answer is provided, it can't be something like Ponders End or Harlow New Town. Some of the situations in which we find ourselves are indeed geographical ones; but others are economic, social or moral. We may still wish to speak of the destination of life's journey; but with the reservation (preferably consciously made) that it is not a destination in the same way as Ponders End.

4 THE AIMS OF EDUCATION

The sort of things we aim at in the literal sense are the cat on the garden wall, the coconut at the fairground, and the double twenty at the local. If we wish to use one word to refer indifferently to the cat, the coconut and the double twenty, we speak of targets rather than aims. And, just as we speak of a journey which is not a journey across the surface of the earth, so also we speak of aiming where what we aim at is not in the literal sense a target. And, in this more extended use, we speak of aims rather than targets

D

(though occasionally we retain the old term, as in 'production targets'). So the existence of the metaphor is made slightly more obvious by replacing the question 'what are the aims of education?' by 'what are those engaged in the activity of education aiming at?' What is being compared in the metaphor is, on the one hand, the relationship between those engaged in education and something else (referred to as the aims of education) and, on the other, the relationship between those who aim at targets (in the literal sense) and the targets at which they aim. It would be wrong no doubt to suggest that those who use this way of speaking have in mind a mental image of a (red, white and blue) bull's eye; nevertheless there is a danger of tacitly assuming that the logic of the one relationship is the same as the logic of the other.

The logic of 'aiming' can best be brought out by considering a distinction which Professor Ryle makes between TASK WORDS and ACHIEVEMENT WORDS. Compare:

'Tiggy Bromsgrove rode in the 3.30'

with 'Tiggy Bromsgrove won the 3.30'.

Certainly Tiggy could not have won the race if he had not ridden in it; on the other hand, he could have ridden in it without winning it. It looks, therefore, as though when he won the race he did two things; he rode in the race and he won the race. But this is misleading, since winning a race is not doing something in the sense in which riding in it is. What we have got is not descriptions of two things that he did, but two descriptions of one thing that he did. The second description covers the same ground as the first, but it adds something to it; not only did he try to win the race, but his efforts met with success. But they met with success not because he did something extra besides trying to win the race, but because he got to the tape before the other horses. Ryle marks the distinction by calling 'running' a task word and 'winning' an achievement word.

In some cases, the distinction between the task and the achievement is even more clearly recognised in our normal ways of speech; compare, for example 'Jones tried to kill Bloggs' and 'Jones murdered Bloggs'. But in many important cases the distinction is less clearly marked; we may even use the same word, alternatively with success written in, and without it. We say Macbeth saw a dagger; but there was no dagger, so how could he see a dagger that wasn't there? So to avoid confusion we would have to say he thought he saw a dagger, or perhaps stipulate that we are using the word 'see' in an unusual sense in which to say 'Macbeth saw a dagger' does not commit us to saying whether there was, or was not, a dagger there for Macbeth to see. And first person uses may be even less clear; when you say 'I saw a ghost' or 'I saw an avocet in Cornwall', you are reporting what you thought you saw. But if we assume that there are no ghosts, (or no avocets in Cornwall), you can't succeed in seeing one. So even in a first person use we might say 'I thought I saw a ghost', not 'I saw a ghost'. In the same way, you can't sit in a chair that isn't there – you can't succeed in doing so, though you can try.

How does this apply to 'aiming'? To aim is to *try* to hit something, but it is not necessarily to succeed in doing so. So 'aiming' is a task word, not an achievement word. 'Education' on the other hand is normally used to describe an achievement. So we might say 'He went to a good school, but he is not what you would call educated'. (Though we might say instead 'He had a good education (i.e. went to a good school) but it didn't do him much good'.)

But if 'education' in the phrase 'the aims of education' is taken as an achievement word a difficulty arises. When we speak of aiming at the bull's eye, we allow for the possibility of failing to hit it. But if we talk about the aims of education, don't we rule out the possibility of failing to achieve those aims if 'education' has success written in? There is a sense in which this might not be so; the standard aim of running a race is to win, nevertheless we *can* speak of 'the aim of winning a race' if the winning of the race is regarded as a means to something further. The aim of winning the quarter-final is to get into the semi-final. The aim of winning the semi-final is to get into the final. And the aim of winning the World Cup? Someone *might* produce an answer, e.g. to raise Britain's prestige in the world. But the football enthusiast would regard this as a silly question. Why do you want to win the World Cup? Because it is the World Cup, because the object of the game is to win – that is what football is all about.

In other words, someone must think football is worthwhile, not because winning the World Cup will boost exports, but because football is football. In the same way, the man who, when asked why he climbed Mount Everest, replied 'Because it is there' meant, if he meant anything, 'I climbed it because I wanted to climb it, and not for any other reason whatsoever; i.e. not to see the view from the top, or for the sake of having tea at Buckingham Palace with the Queen.'

So, too, to ask for the aims of education is like saying: When you have educated someone, you have achieved something, succeeded in doing something. But what do you want that kind of success for? The question, 'what are the aims of education?' is interpreted as 'what use is education?', where 'use' means 'what is it instrumental in bringing about?' rather than as 'what are those engaged in the activity of education aiming at?'

Of course, the question 'what use is education?' is a perfectly proper question in itself. A government asked to spend large sums of money on education is entitled to ask 'Can we afford to do so?' And the reply 'can we afford not to do so?' is equally respectable if education is being looked at from the economic point of view. But from the point of view of those engaged in education, the question 'what use is education?' is as pointless as asking the football enthusiast why he wants his team to win, or asking the mountaineer why he wants to climb. To suppose that the instrumental way of looking at education is the only possible way of looking at it is to overlook the fact that education is worthwhile in itself. It is better, for example, to be educated than ignorant, just as it is better to be well-fed than starving, and would still be better even if lean and hungry workers produced more washing machines than plump contented ones.

5 AIMS, PURPOSES AND IDEALS

In this last section, therefore, I will confine myself to consideration of those aims which those who are themselves engaged in education have. And I shall leave out of consideration also those aims, like gaining a modest competence, which do nothing to single out those engaged in education from those who get their modest competence in other ways. What aims must those engaged in education have, if what they are doing is to be properly called 'education' and not something else?

First, why does it seem reasonable to expect an answer to this question? When you aim a rifle or a wet dish-cloth, there should be no difficulty in saying what you are aiming at. On the other hand, if, after firing an arrow and hearing a yell you need to ask 'what have I hit?', you have probably hit something at which you were not aiming. You can't aim, without aiming at something, and you can't aim at something without being aware, in a fairly precise sort of way, of what you are aiming at. So if someone asks you what you are aiming at, you should be able to tell them. Similarly, those engaged in education are not engaged in an 'aimless' activity; they are trying to do something, to succeed at something. It therefore seems appropriate to ask 'what are they trying to do?' or, 'what are they aiming at?'

But it would be misleading to infer from this that it is possible to give a nice, tidy list of aims, to be circulated to all teachers by the Department of Education and Science or by the local authority; and that, given such a list, success or failure could be read off easily and surely, with questions of methods and procedures being important only in so far as they succeed or fail to produce results. At least, such a list would be possible; it might contain items like: 'Heads of secondary modern schools are to obtain the maximum number of passes in GCE' or 'Grammar schools are to get as many open scholarships as possible.' But aims of this sort, if they are taken as offering a complete account of what education is about, are unduly narrow and restrictive. There is nothing wrong with them as proximate goals; but most people would feel that there is more to education than that.

But perhaps the fault lies in using the terminology of 'aims' at all, if anything more is wanted than a factual description of education which could as easily be given by an external observer. What is really required is an account of what the person engaged in the activity sees himself as doing. Only when we know this, which might be called the intentional aspect of the activity, do their actions become intelligible to us. In general, the person best qualified to give this sort of information is the person himself;

what a person says he is doing is in general the best evidence of what he is doing. But when the activity is as sophisticated and complex as education, those engaged in it will not necessarily be able to provide a clear and concise account of what they are doing, even though they may be quite clear that there is more to it than 'just passing exams'. And this difficulty will increase as we pass from fairly specific aims (like 'lasting out till 4 o'clock without braining one of the little. . . .' or raising 'the average reading age of a class of eight-year-olds up to at least six') to giving some account of what the whole thing is about. It might be better, therefore, to abandon the misleading terminology of aims, and use instead terms like 'purposes', 'intentions' and 'ideals' which are tailor-made to talk about the intentional aspect of activities.

Purposive behaviour must be distinguished from behaviour which, though it gives the appearance of purpose, is not in fact so; what might be called directive behaviour. In both cases, the behaviour may be regarded as capable of explanation in terms of the adoption of appropriate means to bring about given ends. And reference to those ends provides an explanation of the behaviour and makes it intelligible to us. But in some cases we wish to say that the means are seen to be appropriate by the creatures employing them, and the ends are genuinely ends which they have. In other cases, it merely happens to be the case that the means are appropriate to what are distinguishable as ends by the way in which behaviour converges on them. A mechanical tortoise or a defence system do no more than ape purposive behaviour; neither has any conception of what it is doing.

Purposes and ideals differ from aims, not only in not embodying any sort of analogy, but in implying a broader perspective, as I have already suggested. Any case of aiming in the literal sense – say a hunter in the Scottish Highlands aiming at a red deer – is clearly also a case of purposive behaviour. Such a person, caught, so to speak, in the act and asked what he was doing, might perfectly properly reply 'Aiming at a red deer.' And this is what he sees himself as doing, not just what he can be seen to be doing. His target is the deer. His aim, in the more generalised sense, is to hit the deer.

In a sense, too, his purpose is to hit the deer. Certainly if after taking careful aim he did in fact hit it, we should say he hit it on purpose; his hitting it was an intended consequence of what he did. And we might, having got this far, decide that we fully understood what he was doing. But we might not; we might say 'I know what he did; what I don't understand is why he did it.' What purpose does it serve; what purpose does *he* see it as serving? He may, for example, if he is somewhat paranoiac, see in red deer some sort of extension of international communism to the animal kingdom; he may wish to say that he is not just killing an animal, but striking a blow for freedom, democracy and the American way of life. In other words, his purpose is not given by pointing to something external to his action, but by giving a further description of it which accords more closely with the way he sees what he is doing. The further description is more general. It gives us more information, not just about what he is doing just now, but about how what he is doing just now fits into the general pattern of his life. It exhibits it, if you like, as part of a way of life. And we could say that we had arrived at the purpose, or the true purpose, of an action when no further more general description of it, acceptable to the agent, is possible. This is the sort of thing we have in mind in locutions like 'a man of fixed purpose', 'a sense of purpose' and 'a common purpose'. To take the last of these, the man in the Scottish Highlands striking a blow for freedom, democracy and the American way of life, might claim a common purpose with an American bomber pilot in South Vietnam or a man throwing stones at Dr Luther King in Chicago or Alabama.

And terms like 'principles' and 'ideals' while belonging with 'purposes' to the vocabulary we use to talk about intentional activities, look even further than 'purposes' beyond the immediate acts, with their proximate goals, which fill the teacher's day. For my ideals are the sort of purposes which I think I ought to have or would like to have, reflecting my idea of how life ought to be lived or what ought to go on in schools. They function to guide, or perhaps assess, my actual conduct. Purposes have a practical ring; the purposes which I have are reflected in what I actually do. Ideals, on the other hand, are the product of reflection. The ideal solution, way of teaching, etc., is the one which, if . . . if I were a better person or teacher than I am, if everything were as I like to think it is, or would like it to be, if the world (or children) were more tractable than it is.

I hope the discussion of a favourite educational metaphor has not been entirely unfruitful; hereafter I will address myself directly to the concept of education, and to those concepts, like knowledge, learning and teaching, most closely related to it.

SUMMARY

1. The philosopher does not nowadays claim any special knowledge about what the aims of education should be, but he is able to offer, through an analysis of the concept of education and related concepts, some help in reaching an understanding of education as a whole.

2. The need for such an understanding has been partly met by the provision of educational metaphors, but, though such metaphors may be helpful, they may also mislead.

3. The metaphor of a journey might be used for this purpose.

4. A metaphor is involved in talk of the aims of education: in the literal sense what we aim at is targets. 'Aiming' is a task word; to aim is to try to hit something, just as to run in a race is to try to win the race. By contrast, 'won' and 'murdered' are achievement words; they signify success in running in a race or in attempting to kill someone. Some words are sometimes used with success implied and sometimes without any such implication; 'teaching' is normally used as a task word, but sometimes as an achievement word; 'education' is normally used as an achievement word, but occasionally as a task word. If 'education' is understood as a task word in the question 'what are the aims of education?', there is a danger of education being regarded as simply instrumental in the achievement of something external to education.

5. It is important to be clear about those aims which are internal to education, i.e. to be clear about what those engaged in education are trying to achieve. It is perhaps more appropriate to speak of their purposes than their aims; 'purposes' are internal to actions, and place the action in a broader perspective.

FURTHER READING

1. For the reasons given in the text, Plato's educational proposals can only be understood in the context of the more general discussion about the ideal state. See Plato (73) and, for a commentary, Cross and Woozley (29). Whitehead (105, chapter 1) seems to me frankly prescriptive, and for that reason goes beyond a strictly philosophical approach as I understand it (though none the worse for that).

2. On metaphor, see Black (19). For the allegory of the cave, see Plato (73, Bk III, chapter 25).

4. On the aims of education, and the concept of education generally, see Peters (72, Part One and 71). On the distinction between task words and achievement words, see Ryle (83, pages 149–53). Scheffler (87, page 69) discusses Ryle's distinction, speaking of 'success' and 'intentional' uses of 'teach' instead of Ryle's terminology of 'task' and 'achievement'. I am not sure that this is helpful, since success in teaching is certainly not achieved by accident; nor is it correct to say that someone who has taught successfully has not done anything. Macbeth's dagger is discussed by Ayer (10, pages 90–1). On activities undertaken for their own sake, see references given in chapter 1 (page 17).

5. On the distinction between directive and purposive behaviour, see Thorpe (95, chapter 1). The concept of action is discussed further in chapter 5, sections 6 and 7 (pages 65–9) and chapter 8, section 2 (pages 114–16).

5 Education

Earlier, I contrasted activities which aim at a practical result with those which aim at a theoretical result, suggesting that education was an activity of the former sort. And it seems trivial to point out that the practical result aimed at in education is that someone should become educated. But at least it follows, if this is accepted, that there are two parties involved in education: those who are doing the educating and those who are being educated. In talking of the problems facing those engaged in education, and of the aims of education, we are, of course, thinking of those who are doing the educating, not those who are being educated.

If we are prepared to confine the use of the term 'education' to what goes on in schools and other formal institutions of education, this is not misleading. Children go to school to become educated and teachers go to educate them; clearly there are two parties here. But, in fact, a great deal of a child's education takes place outside school, much of it before the child becomes of school age; and I don't wish to be led to ignore this by adopting an unduly narrow concept of education. To put it another way, I don't think it is part of the concept of education that both the parties whom I distinguished should be represented. I propose, therefore, to distinguish FORMAL EDUCATION, in which two parties can be distinguished, and in which one party accepts responsibility for the education of the other, from INFORMAL EDUCATION, in which this condition is not met. I will try to offer an account of 'education' which covers both these cases and then go on to consider the further complications which come with formal education when, comparatively late in the day, the teacher takes over.

2 THE SOCIAL CONTEXT OF EDUCATION

Long ago Aristotle pointed out that man can realise his true nature only in a civil and political society. He had in mind primarily the Greek city-state; but the point can be generalised. Most of the important things which we want to say about people – that they are clever or good, stupid or ignorant, that they are fashion models or pop singers, preachers or pornographers, only make sense on the assumption that we are saying them about people who live in social groups. In particular, if men did not form societies or social groups there would be no such thing as becoming educated. One cannot, therefore, hope to understand the concept of education except in the light of a prior understanding of the concept of society.

Attempts to understand the concept of society have often taken the form of comparisons between man in what has been called the *state of nature* and man in society. Of course, the various accounts offered of the state of nature were not based on observation. Rather the state of nature was hypothetical, arrived at by a process of abstraction. The social contract theorists started with what was known so familiarly that it would have seemed odd to speak of observation; that is, with our ordinary experience of social living. From this, they took away that part of man's existence and experience which, they supposed, he owes to the fact that he lives in society; and were left with their account of the state of nature. If you take away political power – the power to make and enforce laws – you get Locke's state of nature; if you take away morality also, you get Hobbes'. The question with which social contract theorists were directly concerned was the source of political obligation, i.e. our obligation to obey the government and the laws the government makes. It was, they said, as though we had entered into a contract, agreeing to obey the government in return for the benefits which society brings. But such an argument could only start from our ordinary experience of social living, and led, therefore, to a more explicit understanding of that experience.

Something like the transition from a state of nature to a social state takes place during the life of every human being. The new-born baby is no more than a young specimen of the biological species *homo sapiens*. It has to learn to become a person after birth. No one is born a typical American boy or a Merseyside docker. These are things which they have to learn to become; though, of course, which they learn to become depends on the social context into which they are born. Human beings, in fact, have to learn to become people and they can only do so if given the opportunity to do so. A human baby reared by wolves grows into something more closely resembling a wolf than a human being, and a chimpanzee reared in a psychologist's home becomes, within the limits placed upon it by its capacity to learn, like a human child.

To become educated, then, is to be successful in learning to become a person. To give an account of the concept of education, therefore, I shall have to say what is meant here by 'person' (if, that is, purely biological criteria, such as morphology, are rejected as an account of the meaning of 'person') and then go on to give an account of the concept of learning. What is it to learn something, and what is it that has to be learnt in order to become a person?

3 HAVING A CONCEPTION OF REALITY

Persons essentially have some conception of the world they live in and of themselves and of their place in that world.

To have a conception of the world is to see the world as displaying a certain order; to see it as displaying recurring features and as containing objects with enduring identity. The colour red, for example, recurs in tomatoes, flags and bullfinches; sandpaper and cement are both rough to the touch; porcupines and pins are both sharp. And the objects in which these qualities are instantiated are equally varied; we see the world as containing sticks and stones, water and sand, plants and animals, wind, sunshine and rain, green fields and hard ground.

I am talking here not about the world in itself as a reality behind, but also beyond, all our experience; but the world as we see and experience it, and which forms a possible object of knowledge for us. Of course, if the world really were in a state of constant flux, as Heraclitus supposed, then it would not be possible for us to see it as ordered. We could not experience an order which was not there to be experienced. The way the world is limits the possibilities of experience open to us. But what is not so obvious is that the possibilities of experience open to us are limited also by the concepts which we have. The conception of the world we acquire necessarily involves a degree of abstraction; it is not a conception of the world as it is at a moment of time, of something unique, but of the world as containing certain sorts of qualities and things, which can enter into certain sorts of arrangements. The more discriminations we make, the more complex our conception of the world and the wider the range of experiences open to us.

The best evidence of how someone sees the world is provided by what he says about it; use of language is the least equivocal test of whether someone has a concept of the world and of what his conception of it is. But it is not the only test; it seems at least to make sense to suppose that non-language-users, as most or all animals are, possess concepts. Rats, for example, can learn to discriminate between doors labelled with either a circle or a triangle, and this cannot be explained simply in terms of responses to stimuli defined in purely physical terms, since the physical properties of the circle and the triangle can be varied within wide limits without affecting the rats' ability to make the discrimination. Triangles, for example, can come in various shapes, sizes and colours, and can be left as outlines or blocked in; all, in fact, that one triangle has in common with other triangles is its triangularity.

Nevertheless, though the possession of language is not a necessary condition of having a conception of the world, it certainly is necessary to having the rich and varied conception which goes with being a person. Consider, for example, the child who claims to be being followed by a red lion; one which can't be seen (since it is an invisible red lion), but which can be fled from, hence providing the game. You can't claim to be being followed by a red lion unless you know what a red lion is; that is, unless you have the concept of a red lion, which is itself an aspect of having a conception of reality. Having a conception of a reality is not just having a conception of what the world contains, but of the sorts of things it contains. It contains red things and lions, though not red lions and certainly not invisible red lions. But though it doesn't contain invisible red lions, ones which, though you couldn't see them, you could hear growl and perhaps feel their fetid breath on your ankles and which would be as fierce as the flames of hell, we can suppose that it might do so. Invisible red lions are the *sort* of thing the world contains; we can have a concept of an invisible red lion. But how could such a concept be acquired and, if acquired, displayed by a non-language-user? The concept of redness can be acquired by coming into contact with red objects; and this a rat might do as well as a child, provided it had the necessary receptor capacity. But neither rat nor child can acquire the concept of an invisible red lion by coming into contact with one, because there aren't any. There seems no way in which a non-language-user could come to entertain such a notion, and no behaviour which could possibly lead us to suppose that it did. In order to play the game of being chased by an invisible red lion, you have first to include invisible red lions in your conception of the sorts of things which the world might contain, and then act as though you believed that you were being chased by one. And, though a rat might run a thousand miles, we would never conclude that it was pretending to be chased by an invisible red lion, unless it actually said so; and rats don't, as a matter of fact, say anything.

4 THE SOCIAL WORLD

In order to become a person the child has to acquire not only a conception of the physical world, but also of the social world. It must learn to distinguish part of its environment as consisting of persons; it has to acquire, though by gradual stages, the concept of a person. One who fails in this respect – a genuine psychotic – is to that extent less than human. For one important aspect of the concept of a person is that it is essentially a moral concept. People possess physical bodies, but they are not merely physical bodies of a particular shape, texture, etc.; people object to being kicked, for example, though the floor doesn't object to being stamped on (and neither does Teddy, poor chap); and the fact that people object to being kicked is a reason why they shouldn't be kicked. Equally important is the acquisition of a sense of personal identity; the realisation by the child that it is itself a member of the class of persons. As such, the child has the right to be treated with the same consideration which he is expected to extend to others.

Neither the physical world nor the social world are conceived of as static; change cannot be absent from a world which it makes sense to talk of as displaying recurring features and objects with enduring identity. The interaction of objects in the physical world is governed by causal laws; if you drop a cup it breaks, if you shake a rattle it makes a noise. But the relationships between people are of a logically different kind; people are related to one another not by causal laws but by social rules. Such rules have to be learnt (though the cup doesn't have to learn to break when dropped) and, even when learnt, may be ignored on occasion. Most of the more important social relationships, at least, are internal to their terms, in a way in which relationships between physical objects are not. The cup which is on the saucer would still be a cup even if it were not on the saucer. But being a father, or a husband, with the duties and responsibilities which this entails, necessarily involves being related to others (children, or wife); if the relationship is terminated, a man ceases to be a father or a husband.

The pervasive character of the social rules which govern behaviour is shown by the fact that eating is not merely getting nourishment into the digestive system. The child has to learn to take its nourishment in the accepted way; a handful of beans smeared across the face may do the trick, but apart from considerations of efficiency, that is not the way it is done at the Dorchester. Some ways of getting food into the digestive system are acceptable; others are not.

5 PERSONS, ANIMALS AND MEN

I am trying to offer an account of what it is to be a person which does not rely on purely biological criteria. In fact, we do tend to accept only human beings, that is members of the biological species *homo sapiens*, as persons. And it is true that allocation to a biological species is mainly on the basis of physiological and anatomical features, grossly abnormal cases being classed with the species of origin. Men, very roughly, have two legs for walking on and two arms with hands capable of grasping; and are distinguished from other primates by more detailed criteria such as the absence of hair on the body and so on. But a person, as I have used the term, is not someone distinguished in this way, but in the way I have tried to explain. What is important about persons is that they possess a conception of the world and that that conception comes up to minimum standards of sophistication. The most important of the sophistications which I have mentioned are recognition by persons of themselves as members of a class, all of whom are entitled to be treated with moral consideration; and the possibilities, including the possibility of knowledge, which come with language.

It follows from the account which I have given, therefore, that we might easily come to recognise some of the higher animals, such as chimpanzees or porpoises, as persons. Once one has made it clear what is to count as a person it is an empirical matter which sorts of creature satisfy the requirements laid down. And the requirements as I have suggested them make no reference to shape or appearance or even to manner of origin; creatures from other planets who differed grossly from ourselves in appearance could, therefore, count as persons, as could artefacts (robots) made by ourselves on very different principles from ourselves.

Although I have tried to make a sharp distinction between the *concept* of a person and that of a non-person, there will inevitably be many cases in practice where it is not clear whether a particular candidate is or is not to count as a person; that is, whether the concept of a person is properly applied to a particular individual or class of individuals. I do not want anything I have said (either in previous sections or the rest of this chapter) to be taken as implying that I think that there is a sharp distinction in practice between animals and men; especially since, in section seven (pages 67–9), I have assumed for simplicity of exposition that the line of division between animals and men is the same as that between persons and non-persons. If this *is* so it is an empirical matter to be decided by evidence and investigation; it is not something which follows necessarily from the meaning of the terms.

6 POSSIBILITIES OPENED UP BY THE POSSESSION OF A CONCEPTUAL SCHEME

The possibilities opened up by the possession of a conceptual scheme are twofold: theoretical (i.e. connected with truth, as in the theoretical activities which I distinguished earlier); and practical (i.e. connected with the possibility of action, of being active in relation to the world as conceived by me).

I have already stressed that having a conception of the world necessarily involves a degree of abstraction. An actual cat is not, of course, an abstraction; but my seeing it as a cat involves my seeing it as a member of a class of things of which there may be, though there need not actually be, other members. Given then that I have the concept of a cat, and also of a mat, and know also what relationship is involved when one thing is on another, I can suppose that the cat is on the mat, whether the cat is actually on the mat or not. In other words, if I can conceive of the possibility of the cat being on the mat, I may also suppose that this possibility is realised. I can *believe* that the cat is on the mat. Belief is the theoretical possibility opened up by the possession of a conceptual scheme. Of the possible states of affairs which might obtain in front of the fire, the one which I believe actually obtains is that of the mat being occupied by the cat.

On this account, it makes sense to attribute beliefs to animals; just as I said it made sense to say that animals possessed concepts. The monkey who has seen a grape placed under a cup believes that there is a grape under the cup, and when it lifts the cup it expects to find a grape there. When instead it finds a piece of lettuce, substituted for the grape by a scheming psychologist, it is disappointed and angry. The monkey is disappointed because it does not get a grape; but 'because' here does not refer to a causal connection. Rather, failure to get the grape is the reason why the monkey is angry.

So, in exceptional cases, we feel justified in attributing beliefs to non-language-users. But again, the best and most obvious indi-

E

cation of what people believe to be the case is provided by what they assert to be the case and only language-users assert anything. One who is prepared to put forward 'The cat is on the mat' as a true account of the location of the cat, is, in general, taken to believe that the cat is on the mat. Our beliefs are best expressed by those statements which we accept as offering a true account of the world. I will return to the connection between 'belief' and 'truth' later.

The second possibility opened up by the possession of a conceptual scheme is the possibility of action. Just as I can believe that the cat is on the mat provided I possess the relevant concepts, whether or not the cat is actually on the mat, so also I can suppose that the cat which is on the mat might not be. I can conceive of the cat's being on the garden wall or perhaps at the end of my boot. The concept of a person is the concept of one who not only has beliefs about the way the world is, but who is capable of being active in relation to the world and who is so for at least part of the time. Part of the notion of a person is the notion of an agent, one who does things, as well as being the subject of happenings, and who sees himself as capable of doing things. Doing something in this sense involves being aware of one's situation and of oneself in that situation and of the possibility (which only sometimes obtains) of altering that situation in respects which are chosen by the agent. Thus an action involves not merely the agent's knowing what he is doing; what is done is done with the intention of bringing about a certain result, of altering the situation in ways which are foreseen by the agent. The agent exercises choice in doing what he does; what is done is done for a reason. The reason may not extend beyond the direct result intended by the agent; picking up a pebble on the beach may be a trivial sort of action, but if it is an action at all the agent intends the pebble to rest in his hand rather than on the beach. But many of the actions which we perform are not of this isolated, trivial sort; many are done in order to bring about some further result. Such actions are only theoretically discrete; one follows from another and leads to a further action, the whole forming a general pattern or design. Such actions only become fully intelligible to us when we are aware of the general pattern into which they fit. Activities like gardening (and education, too) are made up of whole series of subsidiary actions; cutting the grass, planting seeds, distributing slug pellets, watering the flowers. The slug pellets are distributed to kill the slugs, the slugs are killed because they will eat the young plants, and the seeds were planted in order to grow the young plants, and so on. Gardening itself is undertaken for exercise, to present a tidy front to the neighbours, for the pleasure of seeing things grow, because of the enjoyment flowers provide, and so on.

So in exercising choice I 'shape' my life; my choices reflect my preference for this rather than that; they indicate those things which I consider to be of value. To understand an activity like education we must look beyond the individual acts which teachers perform – like sharpening pencils – and look at the broad context in which they occur; just as, in the previous chapter, I tried to look beyond what the hunter in the Scottish Highlands could be seen to be doing, and to relate that particular action to a broader context.

7 REASONS, CAUSES, AND THE NOTION OF CHOICE

In other words, what comes with the acquisition of a conceptual scheme is at least the possibility of the application of the notion of *choice*.

Persons have some conception of what they are doing and therefore have some conception of what it would have been like to have done something different. Breathing, for example, is something we can choose to do, provided we know what breathing is. Usually we breathe in much the same way as animals, without giving it a thought; but, within limits, we can control the rate at which we breathe and, within more severe limits, whether we breathe at all. And, of course, the movements of our limbs are more easily controlled by us, the beating of our hearts less so. Animals, on the other hand, respond to the forces acting on them in ways which differ only in complexity from the interaction of physical bodies or the inter-reaction of one chemical substance with another. Of course, living matter has properties not shared by non-living; living things are complexly organised to preserve their individual identity and to reproduce their kind; but they are still part of the physical world. And human beings, in acquiring a conception of the world, do not thereby cease to be part of the physical world, and to be subject to the universal natural laws which govern the physical world.

So perhaps Descartes was right in suggesting that animals are no more than complex machines. Man too has a body, which works on much the same principles as the body of an animal. Nevertheless, Hobbes was wrong to suggest that man too is nothing but a machine. But the temptation to make this move is obvious. For what a man does, or hears, or sees, or says, involves the use of his body, and what happens to his body is governed by the same physical laws which govern the rest of the natural world. But in saying that the notions of choosing and deciding have application, we do seem committed to denying that causal laws can also apply to the same phenomenon. The problem of the freedom of the will has been traditionally 'solved' by postulating a *mental substance* (soul or mind) which is added to the physical body which men have; but in analysing what is meant by 'mind' one gets back to notions like 'choice', 'understanding' and 'being aware of what one is doing'. The problem, therefore, is to give an account of 'choice' and related concepts which does not result in any inconsistency in saying, of the same thing, that it is both capable of exercising choice and is nevertheless subject to causal laws.

This is a problem which it would be foolish for me to attempt to solve here. I will confine myself to a few remarks about 'causes' and 'reasons'. The distinction between a cause and a reason is related to the difference between doing something (the notion of agency which I have said is an important part of what is involved in saying that someone is a person) and something's happening to something. Reference to a cause provides an explanation of why somebody did something. And one way of denying that the notion of 'choice' has application (of denying, that is, that we have free-will) is to deny that the distinction between reasons and causes can be maintained. What we take to be reasons, it is said, are merely causes; the stone falling through the air might be supposed to 'think' that it has chosen to fall as it

does, though we know that its movements are wholly determined by the laws of mechanics. The suggestion, which gathers
strength from Freudian theory, is that there is a causal explanation
for all our actions. But giving a causal explanation is itself a case
of doing something and it is essential to the notion of 'explanation'
that reasons can be given for or against it. The notion of 'causal
explanation' itself presupposes the possibility of giving genuine
reasons in support of a particular explanation. The possibility of
justification is essential to the notion of explanation. To show
that a scientist has put forward a certain theory as a result of
hypnosis, or because of a childhood experience, or of his position
in the class structure, is to discredit its status as a candidate for
serious consideration and examination, since it is to undermine
the standard assumption that he puts it forward because he had
good evidence for it.

8 THE IMPORTANCE OF MAKING THE RIGHT CHOICES

I have suggested that the possession of a conceptual scheme
opens up the possibilities, firstly, of belief and, secondly, of action.
And I connected action with choosing between alternative
states of affairs which are conceived of as possible states of affairs.
So part of learning to be a person involves getting into a position
in which choice become possible.

But education involves more than this. It involves not merely
coming to make choices, but coming to make certain choices
rather than others, i.e. making the right choices. The concept
of education has a reference to values built-in because the concept of a person (or a human being) has values built-in. What those
values are will depend on the particular society; there need not
be any choices which are the right choices to make in any absolute
sense. Nor are all the choices which a child learns to make equally
important. Some are mere matters of taste, like not eating cu-
cumber because you don't like it, but others are concerned with
its status as a human being living in a particular social environment. A Western European may be expected to come to share
John Stuart Mill's preference for 'the pleasures of the intellect,

of the feelings and imagination, and of the moral sentiments' to which he attached 'a much higher value as pleasures than to those of mere sensation'; but perhaps the values acquired by an educated Arabian at the time of Scheherazade were very different.

The choices which a child comes to make will depend on a variety of factors; personality factors, chance influences from other people, deliberate attempts by others to influence our choices for their own advantage and so on. The values passed on in education are passed on intentionally by those engaged in education because they are thought to be worthwhile in themselves. For one thing, all education is necessarily also moral education; for another, there are the choices reflected in the curriculum. The question of whether, and if so how, such choices are to be justified is a natural and important one to raise; it is also a difficult one to answer. I shall have very little to say on this subject, because it receives separate treatment in another volume in this series; though I do say a little about the preference for rational over non-rational teaching methods.

I have said that the concept of education has values built in, since to become educated is to learn to be a person and the concept of a person has values built in. In saying, for example, that learning to talk is part of a child's education, while learning to wiggle its ears is not, we are committed to regarding the former accomplishment as of value, while regarding the latter as comparatively trivial. Things like learning to talk and learning to walk seem so basic to any form of human life that it is difficult to imagine a society in which they were not valued. We don't normally think of learning to walk as part of a child's education because walking is usually a matter of maturation rather than learning; but I think that the ability to move about is so important to every aspect of a person's life that if someone did not learn to walk without help we would think it important to teach them.

But there is plenty of room for disagreement about many of the values which are passed on in education. Can you really be educated, someone might say, without a knowledge of classical languages or, a more up to date example, without some knowledge of relativity theory? The term 'education' is often used to include a reference to particular values. But I think this is unfortunate; it results in a culture-bound concept of education; and we do want to allow the possibility that someone might become educated in a society other than our own. To deny this is to suppose that our values are the only possible values and that, therefore, those who do not share them with us are wrong. I think there would be a gain in clarity, therefore, in not incorporating a reference to specific values in the concept of education; in speaking, for example, of a member of the Hitler youth as being educated, though certainly making it clear that we do not share the values which that particular sort of education endorses. We might, for example, qualify our statement with a remark like: 'though what they call "education" is very different from what we call "education" '.

SUMMARY

1. The chapter tries to give an account of the concept of education which includes both formal education (in which two parties, teacher and pupil, can be distinguished) and informal education (in which this condition is not met).

2. The concept of education can only be understood in the light of a prior understanding of the concept of society. The new-born child has to learn to become a (social) person; to succeed in doing this is to become educated.

3. Part of being a person is having a conception of the world, i.e. seeing the world as containing certain sorts of things arranged in certain sorts of ways. Possession of language is not a necessary condition of having such a conception, but it provides the best evidence for saying that someone has a conception of the world, and of what that conception is like. The experiences open to us are limited by the concepts which we have.

4. The child has to acquire a conception of the social world as well as the physical world; of the world as containing persons as well as physical objects. Relationships between persons are of a fundamentally different character from those which obtain between physical objects.

5. The distinction between persons and non-persons is not based on bodily features; it cannot, therefore, be assumed that no non-human beings satisfy the requirements for being a person.

6. The possession of a conceptual scheme opens up the theoretical possibility of belief and the practical possibility of action. In belief, what is conceived of as a possible state of affairs is taken to reflect accurately the way things are in the world. In action, the agent takes steps to bring about a change in the way things are in the world, in accordance with an alternative state of affairs conceived by him.

7. We normally suppose that those whom we say are persons are able to exercise choice. But persons have bodies which are part of the physical world and subject, therefore, to the laws which govern the physical world. This gives rise to the problem of the freedom of the will; some light is thrown on this problem by considering the distinction between reasons and causes.

8. To be educated is not merely to be capable of choice, but to make certain choices rather than others. It is, however, perhaps better not to include a reference to any particular values in the concept of education itself.

FURTHER READING

1. The distinction I have made between formal and informal education is not, of course, the same as the distinction sometimes made between formal and informal teaching methods. Peters' (71) account of the concept of education excludes what I have called informal education. Self-education – in which someone accepts responsibility for his own learning – would be included under the heading of formal education.

2. For Aristotle, see Aristotle (5) and the commentary by Barker (12). The social contract theorists whom I have in mind are Locke (52), Hobbes (45, especially chapters 13 to 18) and Rousseau (81). For comment, see Gough (37) and the relevant chapters of Plamenatz (78). Sabine (84) is a good history of political theory.

3. On the importance of having a conception of the world, see Winch (106, chapter 1). On the question of what it is to have a concept, see Hamlyn (69, chapter 2, especially page 36 ff.), Geach (35, especially chapter 5) and Barrett (111). See also Price (80). Having concepts is usually more closely connected with the use of language than I have suggested in the text. On universals, see Woozley (109, chapter 4).

4. See Strawson's (94) essay in descriptive metaphysics – which aims 'to lay bare the most general features of our conceptual structure' and to show that material bodies and persons are the 'basic or fundamental particulars' in our conceptual scheme; and Ayer (7, chapter 4).

See also Hart (chapter 8 in 32) on the ascription of rights and responsibilities.

On the internality of social relations, see Winch (106, chapter 5, section 1.)

On the difference between nature and convention (and causal and social laws), see Popper (76, volume 1, chapter 5), Benn and Peters (15, chapter 1, section 2) and Winch (123).

5. The account which I offer of belief here, and later in chapter 6, section 3 (pages 80-3), is by no means the only account which could be offered nor is it the one which would command most general acceptance. Scheffler (86, chapter 4) discusses some of the difficulties involved in giving an account of belief. See Ryle (83, chapter 5) for a dispositional account of belief, also cf. Chisholm (112). On the connection between belief and truth, see Griffiths (114). On the theories of truth, and especially on the correspondence theory (which I am in effect putting forward here and in chapter 3, section 3), see Woozley (109, chapter 6), and Pitcher (75).

The concept of action on which I am relying here is a sharpened, more restrictive one than that of an act, or doing something, in ordinary speech. See Hart (chapter 3 in 67) and Austin, Anscombe, Vesey and Melden in Gustavson (38). On the relationship between belief and action, see MacIntyre (chapter 3 in 51). Powell (79) argues against a close connection between actions and intentions.

6. I ought to point out that the word 'substance' used in the expression 'mental substance' is a technical philosopher's term which has been used in different ways by different philosophers. See Vesey (100, first three chapters), and the book of readings edited by Vesey on the body-mind problem (99).

The problem of free-will is a complex one; I have done no more than draw attention to its existence; see, for example, the discussions in Pears (67), Hook (47) and Berofsky (16). In particular, by no means everyone would agree that acceptance of determinism involves a denial of the possibility of choice; see the discussion of possibility and choice by O'Connor (118).

7. On the connection between education and values see Peters (71). For Mill's preferences, see Mill (55, *Utilitarianism,* chapter 2, and *On Liberty,* chapter 3). On the values built into the concept of man see Berlin (chapter 1 in 51). Atkinson (chapter 8 in 4) puts forward the view that in the absence of agreed 'criteria of truth, cogency and correctness ... morality is a field in which there are irreducible options,' and that therefore there is a dilemma in moral education about which moral views a teacher is justified in putting forward. On the account I have given, the only moral views a teacher is justified in putting for-

ward are those which he holds himself; in fact, he cannot avoid doing so, though by practice rather than precept.

On ethics and education, see Peters (72) and Atkinson's own book in this series.

6 Learning

1 'LEARNING' AND THE PSYCHOLOGIST

So far, I have tried to say what it is that has to be learnt in order to become a person. To complete my account of what it is to become educated I will now go on to offer an account of the concept of learning.

I want to start by looking at a definition of 'learning' offered by a psychologist and to make some comments on it. This is a convenient way to proceed; I hope also to show why psychological learning theory cannot be expected to provide an answer to all the teacher's problems about learning in the classroom. E. R. Hilgard offers the following definition of 'learning':

Learning is the process by which an activity originates or is changed through reacting to an encountered situation, provided that the characteristics of the change in activity cannot be explained on the basis of native response tendencies, maturation, or temporary states of the organism (e.g., fatigue, drugs, etc.).

A preliminary point which emerges from this definition is that the psychologist thinks primarily in terms of behaviour. Moreover, behaviour tends to be thought of in terms of bodily movements; bodily movements can be observed and, according to the behaviouristic tradition in psychology stemming from J. B. Watson, psychology can only become scientific by confining itself to what can be directly observed. The behaviour which is relevant to becoming a person cannot be thought of in such limited terms. It is more like the possibility of action which I said was the practical possibility opened up by the possession of a conceptual scheme. On the account I have given, too, belief has a logical priority over action and certainly cannot be reduced to a mere disposition to act in certain ways. In what follows, therefore, I shall be thinking mainly not in terms of the modification of behaviour but of the acquisition of belief.

The second point I want to make about the definition is that it gives an extremely broad meaning to 'learning'. 'Learning' is used to refer to *any* permanent modification of behaviour as a result of prior experience. But I do not think this is correct: unless the person whose beliefs or behaviour have changed can be said to have achieved a success it will not be correct to say that he has learnt anything. Someone who, as a result of prior experience, has come to believe that the world is flat, or that the moon is made of green cheese, hasn't learnt anything; he has merely acquired certain false beliefs. Nor has he learnt anything if, as a result of exposure to advertising material, he comes to believe that Omo washes whitest unless, as a matter of fact, Omo does wash whitest.

The psychologist does not abstract entirely from considerations of success, but tends to supply them arbitrarily and, therefore, to distract attention from their importance. A psychologist may, for example, set out to train a pigeon to go about with its head stretched in the air in an unnatural way. The pigeon's behaviour is 'shaped' by rewarding successive approximations to the required behaviour until it takes the form which the psychologist wanted it to take. The pigeon is then said to have learnt to go about with its head in the air. But in what sense can it be said to have achieved a success? There are two possible answers to this: firstly, its behaviour has come to conform to the standard set up, arbitrarily, by the experimenter; secondly, what it has learnt to do may be said to be not so much going about with its head in the air, as getting food. And it is certainly not entirely arbitrary to refer to this as a success; the behaviour acquired was the behaviour which paid off for the pigeon in the circumstances. In this case, the circumstances were under the control of the experimenter; but, in nature too, circumstances change in ways which are quite independent of the needs of pigeons. So the term 'learning' might be used to include successful adaptation to the environment; the requirement that something should count as success is met impersonally in terms of viability and survival. The psychologist's concern is not so much with what is learnt as with the way in which it is learnt; the adoption of arbitrary criteria of success is justified, therefore, by the assumption that the way in which the pigeon learns what the experimenter decides it shall learn is the same as the way it adapts to changes in its natural environment. In the experimental situation, certain aspects of the environment and of the experimental subject (such as how hungry it is) are controlled by the experimenter, so that changes in behaviour can be related to changes in the environment. (In this case the most important of these would be the presentation of food.) An attempt can then be made to establish causal connections between changes in the environment and changes in behaviour.

The teacher, however, is not interested, at least directly, in how learning takes place, but in seeing that it does take place and that certain things are learnt rather than others. The criteria of success to be applied to see whether learning has taken place, therefore, are laid down for him by the nature of what it is that has to be learnt. I shall say more about this in discussing teaching (in chapter eight, section five, pages 121-4). The important point for the moment is that psychological learning theory provides no information about the criteria of success relevant to curriculum subjects.

My last point is related to the previous one. Hilgard's definition begins: 'Learning is the process . . .'. I do not think that learning is a process (or, to put it another way, that 'learning' is the name of a process). The psychologist, as I have said, tends to supply criteria of successful learning arbitrarily and, therefore, to minimise their importance. He is not concerned to bring about any particular bit of learning, but to investigate the way in which learning takes place. His interest, in other words, is in the learning process, and obviously, if learning takes place, there must be some way in which it comes about. But I think it would be very misleading to identify learning with any process by which learning occurs; to suppose, that is, that 'learning' is the name of a process. The term 'learning' is itself neutral as to what process, or indeed as to whether any process is involved; it simply refers to the fact that a change in belief or behaviour is to count as a success or achievement. It is important to distinguish between the process by which learning takes place (which in the example given above might be called 'conditioning') and the learning itself. This distinction gains support from ordinary usage; the word 'learning' can be used correctly even by those who regard the way in which learning occurs as a complete mystery. 'Conditioning', on the other hand, is a term used by psychologists to refer to one way (or a number of ways) in which changes in behaviour can be brought about; its correct use, therefore, involves some knowledge of psychology.

On this account, then, no restrictions on the way in which learning is to be brought about follow from the meaning of 'learning' itself. But some restrictions are imposed by the relevant criteria of success; that is, by what has to be learnt. In the next section I will try to explain what I mean by calling 'conditioning' a process (and, therefore, what is involved in denying that learning is a process). In the section after that I will suggest that a restriction follows from this as to the way in which rational beliefs may be acquired.

2 CONDITIONING AS A PROCESS

'Conditioning' is the name of a process whereby something happens to something. The contrast between something's happening to something and someone's doing something, is one to which I have already referred (in chapter five, section six, page 66), and one to which I will refer again in discussing teaching as an activity. I think that learning can occur as a result of someone's doing something, as well as a result of something happening to them. But for the moment I shall concentrate on the latter possibility; 'conditioning' is the name of a process, but what *is* a process?

By PROCESS I simply mean to refer to what it is which happens to something in order to change it, provided 'what happens to something' or someone is understood to be contrasted with what they do, as I have indicated above. The changes which occur are likely to be of two kinds, which I will call MORPHOLOGICAL and BEHAVIOURAL. In biology, animals are usually classified by reference to bodily characteristics such as their size, shape and colour; in the case of closely related species, reliance sometimes has to be placed on features which are not obvious on casual inspection, such as details of bone structure. Such bodily features constitute the morphology of the animal and offer a convenient way of classifying it. Of course, animals whose form differs as widely as, say, a cat and an elephant will also behave differently; one has only to imagine an elephant, even a baby one, playing with a ball of wool to realise this. In some cases, two different species of animal, perhaps, could be distinguished only on the basis of behaviour; two species of birds, for example, on the basis of their characteristically different song or behaviour in flight. A classification based on such behavioural features would have to rule out the possibility that they were due to learning, and one would also be inclined to suspect that such differences in behaviour must be due to some morphological feature, even if only at the level of the chromosome. But I hope I have said enough to show that what is meant by morphological changes is independent of what is meant by behavioural changes; even though the two sorts of change may be causally related.

The notion of 'behaviour' here is of course not that of someone's doing something, but rather that of bodily movements produced by the action of external stimuli thought of in physical terms. The force of the contrast I am trying to make may be brought out by applying the notion of a process where it most obviously belongs, i.e. to physical objects. A piece of wood may be processed by being turned on a lathe; the process involved might be called 'turning'. The morphological change brought about by the process is that the shape of the wood (as well, of course, as its overall mass) is different. It may have started as a parallelepiped and ended up in the shape of a propeller. The behavioural change brought about (apart from its behaviour in a spring-balance) is that it now responds to certain stimuli, such as currents of air, differently.

Animals may be processed in a similar way. Buffalo can be turned into biltong, herrings into kippers, and bulls into Oxo cubes. Not only is their appearance changed, but also their response to external stimuli. The biltong is resistant to bacteriological decay; Oxo cubes dissolve in water. In the case of conditioning there is at least no observable morphological change, but the animal responds differently to external forces operating upon it. The psychologist interested in saying how such behavioural changes have been brought about will tend to assume that there must have been some change in the physical or bio-chemical structure of the animal, but that such changes have taken place internally and do not affect the observable form of the animal. Indeed, some psychological learning theories take the form of an account of such changes, the details of which are inferred from all the available evidence, including knowledge of the central nervous system as well as observations of overt behaviour. Some psychologists (especially B. F. Skinner) deny any interest in what goes on inside the animal and confine themselves to the attempt to relate external stimuli to overt behaviour.

'Conditioning,' then, is the name of a process whereby, as a result of an interaction between a living organism and certain external stimuli, future interactions between that organism and similar stimuli take on a different form. Anybody who is prepared to grant anything like a certificate of success in these circumstances is also justified in saying that learning has taken place.

I do not wish to deny that something like conditioning must play a part in human learning; otherwise it is difficult to see how the whole complex business could ever get off the ground. But I wish to deny that conditioning is the only way in which human learning is brought about. In fact, a great deal of what has to be learnt in becoming a person could not possibly be brought about in this way.

3 THE ACQUISITION OF BELIEFS

No restriction, I have suggested, is placed on the way in which learning comes about by the meaning of 'learning', but restrictions do follow from the nature of what it is that has to be learnt. I have suggested that in order to become a person a child has to acquire a conception of the world and some beliefs about the world. Since the possibilities of belief open to us are limited by the concepts which we have, concepts have a logical priority over beliefs. It does not follow from this that they have a temporal or psychological priority; no doubt concepts and beliefs which embody them are acquired *pari passu* by the young child. I will say nothing about the acquisition of concepts, because I do not know what to say about it in the present connection. But I do wish to argue that at least some of our beliefs about the world must be acquired other than as a result of any process such as conditioning. The 'must' here is logical; it could not possibly be the case that all our beliefs are acquired as the result of a process like conditioning.

That this is so follows from two things: the requirement that someone has not learnt anything unless he has got something right; and the nature of belief. The nature of belief imposes restrictions on what can count as success. The psychologist's procedure of determining arbitrarily what counts as success cannot be generalised; for the criteria of success are internally connected with what the success is at. I do not, that is, think it is open to anyone to say that someone who has come to believe that the moon is made of green cheese has learnt anything, because what is required for success in acquiring beliefs about the world is at least that the beliefs acquired should be correct.

This follows from the fact that a belief about the world is not just a conception of the way the world might be, but of the way the world is actually taken to be. I may suppose that there is a tiger in the next room even though I do not believe that there is, for the purpose, perhaps, of providing an example in a philosophical discussion. But what I believe I take to be the case, and those statements by means of which I express my beliefs I offer as true accounts of the world. If I believe that there is a tiger in the next room when in fact there isn't, then I am wrong and the statement whereby I express my belief is false. If I have come to believe that there is a tiger in the next room I have learnt something only if there is in fact a tiger in the next room. If there isn't, I haven't succeeded in doing anything; I have failed. And whether there is a tiger in the next room is not to be determined arbitrarily, but by following standard procedures; that is, by relying on what is sometimes called 'the evidence of the senses': looking and seeing whether there is a tiger there or, perhaps, listening at the keyhole to its ferocious growls. Such procedures are impersonal

F

in the sense that they can be followed by anybody in possession of their faculties; so that, if there is any reason to doubt that the procedure has been properly followed, it can be repeated.

In other words, it is not possible to understand what is meant by 'belief' without realising that in forming a belief I am trying to acquire a conception of the world as it actually is, not as it might have been but isn't. If, therefore, the belief which I acquire is false, I have not succeeded in doing what I took myself to be doing. Of course, somebody else may have succeeded in doing something, but his success is to be judged by criteria other than those relevant to belief. The propagandist, for example, may succeed in obtaining acceptance of false beliefs, but this is a success for propaganda and for the propagandist, not in the acquisition of beliefs and for the person who has acquired the belief.

It is, therefore, essential to the nature of belief that beliefs can be either correct or incorrect, and that the statements which express them are either true or false. But if this is so, then there must be some way of distinguishing between those beliefs which are correct and those which are incorrect, and those statements of belief which are true and those which are false. And if some beliefs are to be judged well-founded and others not so, then someone must have distinguished between them by applying the appropriate procedure. And they, at least, will hold a belief which is correct because they are acquainted with the evidence for that belief; and in that case I will refer to their belief as RATIONAL BELIEF. It is intrinsic to the nature of belief that there exist three possibilities: that what is believed is the case, which I will call TRUE BELIEF; that what is believed is not the case, which I will call FALSE BELIEF; and that a true belief is held because there is evidence for it, which I have called rational belief. The astronaut who believes that the moon is made of green cheese because he has been up there and had a bite believes what he believes because he is acquainted with the evidence for it. His belief is a rational belief.

Some at least of our beliefs must be rational beliefs – held because of the evidence for them. But to come to believe something after examining the evidence for it, and accepting it as a correct belief in the light of that evidence, is not a case of something happening to someone; it is a case of someone's doing something, if anything is. The holding of rational beliefs cannot have been brought about by anything resembling a process, whatever the process may be. This is not to deny that rational beliefs may be acquired through a learning programme based on principles suggested by operant conditioning. But a person who learns in this way is not being conditioned; unless, that is, no more is implied than that a particular method of presentation has been adopted on psychological grounds.

4 BELIEF AND EVIDENCE

I have suggested that unless beliefs were the sort of things which could be correct or incorrect, which in turn could not be the case unless *someone* held some of his beliefs because of the evidence for him, then our concept of belief would be other than it is.

Belief can be brought about by presentation of evidence only if there is evidence available to be produced. Those beliefs which the available evidence does not support are described as false. False beliefs cannot, therefore, be produced by presenting the evidence for them, since the available evidence, if honestly presented, will not support them. Subject to the qualifications in the following paragraph, therefore, false beliefs cannot be held on rational grounds; and, since people do come to hold false beliefs, they must come to hold them in ways other than by becoming acquainted with the evidence for them. And whatever way that can come about, true beliefs can just as easily be acquired in the same way. All beliefs are accepted as true by the believer; none is accepted because of its falsity, since to say 'I believe so-and-so, though so-and-so is not true' would be self-contradictory.

The account which I have given of the relationship between belief and evidence is over-simplified; we do speak of evidence pointing to beliefs which are false and we do allow the possibility that someone may rationally hold what later turns out to be a false belief. But this way of speaking is most appropriate in situations in which we do not know which of two beliefs is true, and are looking at the available evidence, or collecting evidence, to enable us to choose between them. Was it Tiggy Bromsgrove or Teapot Manley who doped the horse? Tiggy was riding it in the race, but Teapot had charge of it in the stables. Tiggy was seen giving the horse something before the race and heard to utter the words 'Now let's see you win', but he swears it was only a lump of sugar. In the end, perhaps, it turns out that the horse was not doped at all, and the vet had only said it had been to discredit Tiggy and Teapot, since Teapot had helped Tiggy elope with the vet's second-best girl friend. So we need to consider all the relevant evidence before deciding which beliefs to accept as true; or to speak retrospectively of the evidence which seemed to favour a particular conclusion, though did not in fact do so. This is what happens when a court of law reaches a decision after all evidence to be taken into account has been offered and assessed. And the position is similar in science; though in science there are no final decisions and the search for evidence goes on indefinitely. As science develops, and the evidence on which scientific beliefs rest are subject to revision and addition, the beliefs which it is rational to hold change. It was, for example, rational for Ptolemy to hold beliefs about the position of the Earth in the universe which it would not be rational for a present-day astronomer to accept. And, of course, one cannot always eliminate doubt; in which case the rational thing would be to suspend belief or hold 'qualified' belief.

I will not here discuss the various ways in which beliefs, true or false, can be produced in ways other than the production of evidence. The techniques used in advertising, propaganda and indoctrination present obvious examples: constant repetition of the belief, assuming that a belief is obviously true and therefore beyond question and so on. In all such cases it is natural to say that the person has been *caused* to have the belief, much as the pigeon was caused to walk about with its head in the air in the conditioning experiment I mentioned earlier. I doubt whether the notion of 'conditioning' is strictly applicable to any case of belief, since what is believed must be understood. But certainly all these methods of producing belief represent a sort of halfway house between conditioning and producing belief by rational means. And the comparison with conditioning is apt because the person who is to acquire the belief is treated not like a rational creature capable of forming his beliefs for himself in the light of the evidence, but like the bull which is transformed into Oxo cubes – something to be operated on by external forces to fulfil purposes which are not his own. I shall have more to say on this subject when discussing teaching.

5 THE IMPORTANCE OF RATIONAL BELIEF

I have suggested that at least some of our beliefs must be held on rational grounds if we are to have any beliefs at all, and also that the acquisition of a belief cannot be described in terms of 'learning' unless the belief is accepted as true. The connection is between the concepts of 'learning' and 'belief' (and so between the concepts of 'learning' and 'true'). It is, therefore, the person who describes the acquisition of a belief in terms of 'learning' – i.e. who considers that the concept of 'learning' has application – who is also committed to acceptance of the truth of the belief. In view of the further connection between 'education' and 'learning', therefore, the beliefs which are acquired in becoming educated must at least be true. But it does not follow from the meaning of 'education' that they must be rational beliefs; if we insist on building in our preference for rational belief into the meaning of 'education' we will end up with a culture-bound concept of education, for that preference expresses a value judgement which may not be shared in societies other than our own.

All that follows from the meaning of 'education' is that somebody in the educational system must be in a position to distinguish between true and false beliefs in the light of the evidence. Otherwise the minimum standard, without which we would not be talking about education at all, cannot be adopted. But it is possible to adopt the point of view that access to the evidence should be the prerogative of a privileged few and that true belief alone is good enough for the masses. Those who have access to the evidence – those, that is, who are in a position to decide which beliefs are true – withhold it from others. They offer to others the possibility of true belief, but deny them what they have themselves, rational belief. Their position is similar to those who impose a censorship on the arts and literature. To decide that a novel is depraved and therefore likely to corrupt, one must first read it. Those who take on the task of censorship are, presumably, not corrupted by reading the novel; nevertheless, they feel justified in supposing that others should be prevented from reading it lest they be corrupted. The censor denies to others what he has had himself: the opportunity to form his own opinion of the novel.

I will try, therefore, to say something about how anyone should be led to adopt such a position and why it should be rejected.

6 THE JUSTIFICATION OF RATIONAL BELIEF AND THE NATURE OF TRUTH

The view of truth as unchanging is one which has always been attractive. If it is true today that I have bright blue eyes, it will be true tomorrow. Of course, a truth of this sort is not timeless, since my eyes may lose their lustre, but it will always be true that I had bright blue eyes today. Again, though I may accept it as true today, tomorrow I may change my mind and decide that they are grey after all. But this, too, can be accommodated to the view that truth is unchanging; it is not that what was true has ceased to be true, but that I was mistaken in what I took to be true. But if it is true today that two and two make four, then it always will be true and always has been true. The truths of mathematics have a timeless quality and seem to wear their truth on their faces, eliminating the possibility of mistake. It is not surprising, therefore, that those who have emphasised the unchanging nature of truth have always tended to regard the truths of mathematics as providing a paradigm by which other truths are to be judged. Plato, for example, looked for truth not in the changing world of appearance, but in mathematics and in a timeless world of Forms.

This view of truth as essentially unchanging is obviously not completely mistaken, but it is misleading if it leads us to think of truth as an absolute, to which we have, or might have access. (Plato, for example thought that we could gain access to absolute truths by becoming acquainted with the world of Forms.) The

word 'true' is properly applied to those statements which we accept
as true; we have, and can have, no access to truths which are
'really' true, and whose truth is, therefore, beyond question. The
truths of mathematics, indeed, turn out to be a poor model,
since they gain their status as unchallenged truths only by saying
nothing; their logical form is no different from the tautologies
of ordinary language like 'A table is a table' which, though true,
tell us nothing. Or at best they are like statements like 'A chair
is used for sitting on', which tells us nothing about the world,
but only something about the meaning of the words used.

What has this to do with the justification of rational belief? One
who had access to absolute truths could be sure that they would
never change; at no time in the future could there be any possible
grounds for withdrawing their status as truths. But if 'true' is
properly applied to those statements about the world which we
accept as true, then truth is not unchanging; at least in the sense
that those statements which we accept today we may reject
tomorrow. But our beliefs – what we accept as the case – can only
change in this way in so far as they are rational beliefs. Beliefs
based on evidence can be revised in the light of fresh evidence
and after fresh examination of existing evidence. Our knowledge
of the world is something which is constantly changing; it is
built up over a period of time, and subject to constant revision and
addition. Of course, there is a connection between 'belief' and
'truth'; but the connection is between the concepts. What we
believe we accept as true, but this is not inconsistent with the
fact that there is a constant revision of those propositions, especially those of the theoretical disciplines like science, history, etc.,
which we accept as true.

It is, therefore, important not merely to pass on the facts, but to
pass on the evidence on which they are based. Indeed, it is often
more important to acquaint people with the *sort* of evidence
which counts for or against a particular belief than to pass on the
belief itself. What is important is not simply to have a true
conception of the world, but to be able to form one for oneself.

The analogy with censorship is reflected here also. If there is
only one correct moral point of view – that of the censor – then
the action of the censor is justified. But if the moral point of

view of those who wish to read forbidden books is as well-founded as his own, then he is guilty of assuming his own infallibility in order to impose his moral prejudices on others. The censor is the moral adult; the rest of us are moral children.

SUMMARY

1. Three points were made about the psychologist's definition of 'learning' as the permanent modification of behaviour as a result of prior experience. Firstly, the psychologist thinks in terms of behaviour rather than belief, and behaviour is thought of in terms of bodily movement. Secondly, the definition does not mention the importance of success; but only if a change in behaviour or belief can be characterised as a success can it be correctly described in terms of 'learning'. Thirdly, 'learning' is not the name of a process at all, though 'conditioning' is.

2. In a process something happens to something, resulting in a change in either its outward shape (i.e. a morphological change) or in its tendency to react to forces acting upon it (i.e. a behavioural change). The change brought about when someone is conditioned is primarily behavioural.

3. Rational beliefs cannot be acquired as a result of being subjected to any process, but only by becoming acquainted with the evidence for the beliefs in question. And some, at least, of our beliefs must be held on rational grounds. Therefore, not all beliefs could possibly be acquired as a result of being subjected to any process.

4. False beliefs cannot be produced by an impartial production of the evidence, since this would lead us to reject them, not to accept them. People commonly persist in holding false beliefs even though there is ample evidence for their falsity. There are ways other than the production of evidence by which beliefs can be produced, such as those used in advertising, propaganda and indoctrination.

5. To suggest that, so far as possible, the beliefs transmitted in education should be rational and not merely true is to put forward a value judgement which requires defending.

6. It will not seem as important to those who look upon truth as something essentially unchanging to pass on rational belief rather than merely true belief in education. For if truth (or what we accept as true) is unchanging, then no one will ever be called upon to revise a

true belief. Beliefs based on evidence, on the other hand – rational beliefs – can be revised in the light of fresh evidence.

FURTHER READING

1. Hilgard's definition of learning is taken from Hilgard (44, page 3). On the concept of behaviour, see Hamlyn (chapter 3 in 26). On logical and psychological aspects of learning, see Hamlyn (chapter 2 in 69).

Scheffler (86, pages 6 and 7) distinguishes a 'tutorial' and a 'discovery' use of 'learnt', the latter only implying the truth of what has been learnt, and seems to attach equal importance to both uses. By contrast, I have taken 'learning' as primarily an epistemological concept. On the difficulties raised by cross-cultural comparisons, which Scheffler's account raises, see Winch (124).

In the text I have not stressed the distinction between classical and operant conditioning. Though there are important differences between them, I do not think they affect the point I am trying to make. In saying this, I am implicitly denying that operant responses can be identified with voluntary behaviour and that all 'voluntary' behaviour is the result of prior (planned or unplanned) operant conditioning. This is consistent with my earlier remarks on the freedom of the will in chapter five, section seven (page 68). One way of denying the distinction between causes and reasons would be to offer an account of the giving of reasons in terms of prior operant conditioning; that is, by reference to a history of reinforcement for that particular operant response.

See Skinner (89 and 91) for embracing claims for the scope of the application of the notion of operant conditioning (and of 'behavioural engineering'). For a discussion of conditioning and learning which arrives, for more technical reasons, at a conclusion similar to my own, see Vesey (chapter 4 in 69).

2. The methodological controversy as to whether the learning theorist should concern himself with what is or might be going on inside the animal is discussed by MacCorquodale and Meehl (117).

3. On the account I have given, there seems no possible way in which the child could start to acquire concepts. If so, there must be some concepts (or 'ideas') which are innate. What is accepted as innate need be no more than a disposition to make certain discriminations due to the inheritance of a particular sort of central nervous system and appropriate receptor capacity.

Hirst's discussion (chapter 3 in 69) of limitations placed on teaching methods by the nature of the subject taught is relevant here.

On belief see references for chapter 5, section 5 (page 73).

Cf. chapter 8, section 6 (pages 124-7) on the connection between teaching methods (i.e. methods of bringing about learning) and rationality, and the remarks about conditioning in section 4 of this chapter (page 84).

4. The connection between evidence, belief and truth is complicated, much more so than the simple account presented in the text suggests. See Kneale (49, especially Part One) and Popper (77, especially chapter 10).

For non-rational methods of producing belief, see Brown (25) and Sargant (85).

5. On censorship, see Anderson (110).

6. For a classic statement of the view of truth as unchanging, see Plato (73, especially chapter 19, also chapters 23, 24 and 25).

The account of the logical status of the truths of mathematics which I mention is not the only possible one. It was put forward by Wittgenstein (108) and was used by the logical positivists to save mathematics from elimination by the verification principle.

7 Knowledge

I THE JUSTIFICATION OF A PHILOSOPHICAL ANALYSIS OF A CONCEPT

In previous chapters I have tried to use the philosophical analysis of language as a way of coming to understand, and of making clear, what those engaged in the practice of education take themselves to be doing. I started by looking at 'education' itself, and was led from there to look at 'person', 'concepts', 'belief', 'truth' and 'evidence' and, in the previous chapter, at 'learning' and its connection with 'belief'. I want now to go on to consider 'knowledge'.

Before doing so, however, I would like to make a few general remarks about the difficulties involved in justifying any proposed analysis of the meaning of a word. It is important at least to recognise these difficulties, since philosophy is essentially a rational activity, and philosophers expect their views to be accepted only in so far as reasons can be produced for doing so. The first and most important consideration I have had in mind is whether the proposed analysis offers an accurate description of the way we normally use the word. The difficulty here is with the word 'normally'; which are the 'normal' uses of a word, and which are the exceptional ones? People use the same word in a variety of contexts, both linguistic and semantic. The burden of meaning which a word carries will depend partly on the context of other words in which it occurs and which constitute its LINGUISTIC CONTEXT. The SEMANTIC CONTEXT is simply the non-linguistic context in which a word is used. The word 'red', for example, is normally used to refer to red objects. But in the situation referred to earlier, in which an invisible red lion wantonly terrified young children, the word 'red' could not be used to refer to the presence of a red object, since the lion was invisible. Calling it 'red', then, could not have had the normal force, but was a way of referring to the fact that the lion was as fierce as the flames of hell.

The difficulty, therefore, in relying on ordinary usage, and pointing to 'what we would ordinarily say' in order to justify a proposed analysis, is that there is no one standard use of the words of ordinary language. In practice, philosophers tend to emphasise certain uses to which a word is put at the expense of others, saying that they are 'central' cases or provide 'paradigms' of the meaning of the word. But the selection of certain paradigms rather than others itself needs justifying, for the philosopher is not so much describing the central use of the word as suggesting that a certain use be regarded as central or primary. I suggested, for example, that 'learning' be understood to imply that someone had got something right, while recognising that we do speak of people learning incorrectly. In suggesting this I was thinking of the educational context in which the word is used; we don't normally want to say that children who get all their answers wrong at the end of year examination have learnt just as much as those who get them right, although they have learnt something different. Rather, we would say that they haven't learnt anything. Again, the distinction which I have stressed between true belief and rational belief may not be reflected in our ordinary way of talking, although it is familiar enough in philosophy. But given the distinction it is then easier to make the point, which one may wish to do, that education is concerned with the transmission of rational belief rather than true belief alone.

2 OUR USE OF THE WORD 'KNOWLEDGE'

The word 'knowledge' is grammatically similar to words like 'bat' and 'ball': words which we call nouns and which normally function as the names of things, such as bats and balls or, at least, if they are not properly thought of as the names of things, they are used to refer to things in order to say something about them. Though this might lead us to suppose that knowledge is a thing, a moment's reflection will allow us to see that it can't be a thing in quite the same way as a bat or a ball; a bat can be picked up or lost, and a ball can be thrown or caught, but we don't expect to be able to do that sort of thing with knowledge. It is tempting, therefore, to say that, though knowledge is not a thing in quite the same way as a bat or a ball, this is not because it is not a thing at all, but because it is a special sort of thing; indeed, we do talk about a 'body of knowledge'. In other words, we might be tempted to suppose that we could understand 'knowledge' on the analogy of 'bat'; and this is attractive because we think we understand what sort of thing a bat is.

But one of the most important features of twentieth century philosophy has been an increasing realisation of the many different ways in which words function. G. E. Moore, for example, thought at the beginning of the century that if 'good' were not the name of a quality in quite the same way as 'yellow', nevertheless it functioned in much the same sort of way. Now, however, we tend to think that the word 'good' functions in an altogether different way from words which are the names of qualities; 'good' means, according to R. M. Hare, what I would choose or recommend others to choose. J. L. Austin, in particular, has drawn attention to the way we use the concept of knowledge, emphasising not the use to which we put the noun 'knowledge' but the verb 'knows'.

My suggestion, then, following Austin, is that we shall understand the concept of knowledge better if we approach it via its occurrence in the verbal form 'knows' rather than the substantive form 'knowledge'. Before doing so, it will be helpful to introduce the notion of a PROPOSITIONAL FUNCTION. A comparison with algebra may help. In the expression '$a + b = c$' the letters a, b and c stand for numbers; so that if we replace the letters by numbers we get an arithmetical expression such as '$2 + 3 = 5$'. In the same way, in the expression 'X knows that p', the capital letter X stands for anyone to whom it would make sense to attribute knowledge and the small letter p stands for the sentence expressing the knowledge attributed to them. If a substitution along these lines were carried out we would get a sentence like 'Tiggy Bromsgrove knows that overwork causes horses to get spavins'.

What I will consider, therefore, is the use to which we put sentences of the form 'X knows that p'.

3 KNOWLEDGE CLAIMS

nce I am considering the *use* to which expressions of the form 'X knows that *p*' are put, it will be as well to bring an explicit reference to the language-user into the picture. If the capital letter Y is used to stand indifferently for any language-user, then we get: 'Y says "X knows that *p*".' Language-users are just the sort of entity to whom it would make sense to attribute knowledge; X and Y could therefore either be the same person, or they could be different persons. If they are the same person, we get a first person use of 'X knows that *p*'; like 'Tiggy Bromsgrove says "I know that overwork causes horses to get spavins" '. If X and Y are different persons, we get a third person use of 'X knows that *p*'; like 'Teapot Manley says "Tiggy Bromsgrove knows that overwork causes horses to get spavins" '. In the first person case, a claim is made by the speaker on his own behalf: in the third person case, the claim made by the speaker is made on behalf of someone else. In the latter case, it would be more natural to say that the speaker is attributing knowledge to someone else, rather than claiming it for himself; but I want to avoid saying that what is claimed or attributed is knowledge. What I wish to say is claimed is that a particular belief which is held is a rational belief, and that we use the concept of knowledge (at least in propositions of the form 'X knows that *p*') to make explicit claims to rational belief.

In insisting that what is claimed is rational belief rather than knowledge, I am making a distinction which is not always made. 'Knowledge' and 'rational belief' are often treated as two names for the same thing. A comparison with A. J. Ayer's account of 'knowledge' may make this clear. Ayer's requirements for knowledge are, firstly, that 'what is known should be true' and, secondly, that 'one should be completely sure of what one knows'. These two requirements alone give something like what I have previously called 'true belief', though they make it clear that the use of 'I believe' to express doubt (as in 'I believe it is five o'clock (but I'm not sure)') is not involved here.

Ayer's first two requirements are not sufficient to give him knowledge, since 'a superstitious person who had inadvertently walked under a ladder might be convinced as a result that he was about to suffer some misfortune; and he might in fact be right. But it would not be correct to say that he knew that this was going to be so.' This is because 'normally we do not say that people know things unless they have followed one of the accredited routes to knowledge. If someone reaches a true conclusion without appearing to have any adequate basis for it, we are likely to say that he does not really know.'

So the addition of this third requirement steps up the requirement for knowledge, in a way which is similar to the requirement that rational belief be based on evidence whereas true belief need not be. The requirement for rational belief is slightly higher, since, on Ayer's account, if someone were repeatedly successful in predicting the results of the 3.30, we might come to say that he knew what the winner was going to be, even though we did not know how he knew. 'We should grant him the right to be sure, simply on the basis of his success.'

The most important way, however, in which the account of 'knowledge' I have tried to suggest differs from Ayer's is in the way in which truth enters into account. Truth enters into Ayer's account directly, since 'what is known should be true'. In the account I have suggested, truth enters not directly, but via belief, since to believe that p is to believe that p is true. And I have then suggested that at least a central use of the verb to know is to put forward a claim on behalf of the speaker or someone else that a particular belief is held on good evidence; that is, that it is a rational belief.

4 KNOWLEDGE AND TRUTH

It is always possible that any statement accepted as true may be false. If, therefore, what is known must be true, can we ever be said to know anything? This is the problem of philosophical scepticism, which I hope I have avoided in the account of knowledge which I have given.

We normally suppose that human knowledge is both a possibility and a possibility which is realised in countless instances; that it is not like love which is 'true just in fairy tales'. I know, for example, that there are five chairs in my room; I know because I have just counted them. But if I have made a mistake – if I have miscounted, or if what I took to be a chair was merely a shadow on the wall – then it is not true that there are five chairs in my room and I cannot, therefore, be said to know that this is so. I believe there are, but I am mistaken. Moreover, in any particular case in which I believe that something is the case, it will always be possible that I am mistaken; the possibility that I have made a mistake cannot be ruled out as inconceivable. It follows from the fact of human fallibility that on any occasion on which I take something to be the case I might be mistaken; what I take to be true may not be true. But if what I know *must* be true, am I ever really justified in claiming to know anything? If the connection between 'knowledge' and 'truth' is as tight as has often been supposed, then I cannot be said to know anything unless even the possibility that I may be wrong has been ruled out. The requirement that what is known must be certainly true, coupled with the suggestion that we can never be certain of the truth of any statement about the world, has led philosophers to express doubts about whether we ever do know anything. Consequently a great deal of history of epistemology (theory of knowledge) has been taken up with attempts to combat scepticism of this sort.

I have tried to avoid this difficulty by suggesting that a principal use of the concept of knowledge is to claim that a belief, held by the speaker, is a rational belief; or to admit that a belief, held by someone else, is a rational belief. The account of knowledge which I have offered allows for the fact of human fallibility, rather than ignoring it, with the consequence that nothing then counts as knowledge. The choice between rejecting an account of knowledge which has this consequence or accepting a consequence which is contrary to what we normally take to be the case (i.e. that human knowledge is both attainable and frequently attained), does not seem to be a difficult one.

5 CHALLENGES TO CLAIMS TO KNOW

Claims made by the use of the verb 'to know' will, in principle, always be open to challenge. The possibility of challenge is recognised by the use of the word 'knows', rather than ruled out by it. There will, of course, be many occasions on which no one is disposed to dispute such a claim. Unless some facts are accepted without dispute it is difficult to see how there could be other facts which are the subject of dispute.

Nevertheless, what is important about claims to know is that they are always open to challenge rather than the fact that they are sometimes accepted without challenge. If X claims to know that p, he is making a perfectly proper use of the word 'knows' even though his claim may be challenged. 'Do you really know?' is a proper response to his claim, provided it is taken as meaning 'Do you really have evidence for your belief that p?' X can meet such a challenge by producing the evidence for his belief, if he has any. If his evidence is accepted as providing rational grounds for believing that p, X's claim to know that p will be admitted, and X's rational belief that p will now be shared by his challenger.

On the other hand, the evidence produced may not be accepted as providing rational grounds for the belief in question. X is then likely to enquire why the grounds which seem adequate to him are not acceptable. If he is satisfied with the reply he receives, he may modify his own beliefs; if, that is, he wishes to retain the rational status of his beliefs, rather than to retain them as mere prejudices. In short, what is likely to occur when a claim to rational belief is challenged is an argument about whether, in the light of the evidence, the belief is entitled to be accepted as true. The challenge 'Do you really know?' can in principle be met, provided it is interpreted as meaning 'Do you really have evidence for your belief that p?'

The question 'Do you really know?' has, however, frequently been interpreted as meaning 'Is what you take to be true on good evidence really true?' On this interpretation, it is not denied that the evidence on which X relies is good evidence, or at least that it is what is normally accepted as good evidence. Nor is it denied that it is the best evidence which it is possible to have; what is being denied is that the best evidence which it is possible to have is good enough. However good the evidence for accepting p as true, there still remains the possibility that p is after all not true. Interpreted in this way, the question 'But do you really know that *p*?' leads to EPISTEMOLOGICAL SCEPTICISM; to a denial, that is, that a claim to knowledge is ever justified, since it sets a standard for empirical knowledge which cannot, in principle, be met. For if the best evidence which it is possible to have is not good enough, how is the truth of any statement to be established?

I have suggested that the problem of scepticism arises out of a mistaken view about the relationship between 'knowledge' and 'truth'. There is, therefore, no need to accept the existence of a problem of scepticism and no need to combat it. It is, however, important for the philosophy of education that the sceptical challenge should be met if it is once admitted. If to be educated is to learn to be a person, and if part of being a person is coming to have some knowledge of the world in which one lives, then education is not possible unless knowledge is possible. To deny that the concept of knowledge has application is, therefore, to deny also that the concept of education has application, since the possibility of knowledge is presupposed by education.

It is, therefore, worth noting that even for those who accept the sceptic's interpretation of the question 'Do you really know?' there are many moves left. Even if it is accepted that no *evidence* is good enough for the truth of any statement, it might still be the case that some statements can be known to be true. We might, for example, have or acquire direct access to a storehouse of timeless truths) something like Plato's world of Forms (and this, of course, incidentally opens up an exalted role for education) since to become educated is to acquire the key to the storehouse). Or there may be some statements which wear their truth on their sleeves, so to speak, and whose truth can therefore be known directly without the need for reliance on evidence. Favourite candidates here would be the truths of mathematics (since no evidence counts for the truth of the statement: 'Two plus two equals four'; its truth follows directly from the meaning of the symbols used); statements like Descartes' 'cogito, ergo sum' (I think, therefore I am) which, for slightly more complicated reasons, cannot but be true if uttered; and reports of direct experience, like 'I am now seeing a red patch', which are taken as reports of what is directly given and which, therefore, leave no room for error. Once the sceptic's question is admitted, however, it is extremely difficult to answer satisfactorily; it is better, therefore, to reject the question out of hand rather than to try to answer it; provided, of course, it can legitimately be rejected.

6 ESTABLISHED KNOWLEDGE

Though I have stressed that any claim to know is, in principle, open to challenge, I have also admitted that there are many statements which no one would be likely to challenge. This is partly due to an uncritical acceptance of beliefs which have been commonly accepted for a very long time. But it is also due to the fact that the evidence for many of our shared beliefs is so obvious that there is little point in one person drawing another's attention to it. Nor is it surprising that a shared body of rational belief tends to grow up in any human society. What it is rational to believe depends on what there is evidence for believing, and what there is evidence for believing is independent of the wishes, wants or convenience of any particular person. On the other hand, the evidence for a belief is, in principle at least, accessible to all. If the cat really is on the mat, anyone who cares to look will see it there, and hear it purr too.

That the evidence for a particular belief is publicly accessible is obvious enough if we confine ourselves to ordinary, everyday beliefs like the belief that the cat is on the mat. And the case is similar if we go from statements about particular cats to statements about all, or most, cats. Cats like milk, dogs like bones; if you hit your thumb with a hammer it will hurt; people get angry if you stick pins in them; and so on. There is a whole host of what might be called common sense beliefs about the world, for which the evidence is easily available to all and which are in consequence very generally accepted without question.

The case is slightly different, however, when we turn to more sophisticated beliefs about the world. There are two sorts of reasons why I may be unable to form a rational belief that horses get spavins through overwork. Firstly, though I know what a horse is, I may not know what a spavin is; I might be unable to recognise one if I saw one. Secondly, even if I knew what spavins were, I might not know how to decide whether spavins are caused by overwork; or, if I know in a rough and ready way the sort of evidence which is relevant, I might be quite unqualified to unearth it.

Countless other, more important, examples might be produced. What are the effects of sensory deprivation? Is it true that the speed of light is constant to the observer? Does the reticular activating formation of the brain control sleeping and waking? What would be the correct value to assign to the multiplier effect in the economies of present-day Germany or Japan? These questions, and thousands like them, only arise in the context of specialised forms of knowledge. Belief of any sort is possible only in so far as one understands the language in terms of which the beliefs are phrased; rational belief is possible only in so far as one is acquainted with the techniques developed in that field for distinguishing between true and false beliefs. Within each of the organised forms of knowledge there does in fact exist a body of established knowledge, but before considering this further I will say a little more about the difference between common sense and formal knowledge.

7 COMMON SENSE AND FORMAL KNOWLEDGE

I do not wish to suggest that the distinction between common sense and formal knowledge is a sharp one. It is on the basis of the common sense, shared conception of the world that more sophisticated concepts are built, bringing with them new possibilities of beliefs about the world and new criteria of truth. Such concepts are specialised, or technical, precisely in the sense that they are not possessed by all members of a society simply because they are members of that society, but only by those who have deliberately gone out of their way to acquire them or who have been given special opportunities for doing so. They are acquired only through the sort of conscious effort and study typically associated with schooling. And this is not surprising, since I am now talking about the 'subjects' of the school curriculum. The acquisition of the concepts in terms of which such subjects are structured will, at least, involve contact with others who already possess them, either directly as in the teaching situation or indirectly through books. But for the moment I am not concerned with the circumstances in which such knowledge is acquired, but with what it is which is acquired.

To be introduced to a new form of knowledge is to see the world in a new way, to extend your conception of reality and to extend the possibilities of experience open to you. New concepts allow the formation of new beliefs, but at the same time create new possibilities of error; since, if we can acquire new beliefs about the world which are true, we may also acquire new beliefs about the world which are false. So it is intrinsic to such new concepts that they bring with them also new criteria of truth, i.e. new ways of distinguishing between those beliefs which are true and those which are false. And, again, knowing what counts for or against such a belief is something which has to be learnt. The evidence for the recession of the galaxies, for example, is hardly even intelligible to most people. At best, one may know that it has something to do with the red shift; but what is the red shift? The photographic plate reproduced in the book doesn't mean anything unless it is interpreted in the right way. Astronomers may be confident that it provides evidence for the recession of the galaxies, but the rest of us have to take their word for it. We do not possess the theoretical background necessary even to understand what the evidence is, and are certainly in no position to form an independent opinion about the strength of it.

8 FORMS OF KNOWLEDGE

Forms of knowledge, then, are distinguished from one another by the directions in which they expand our conception of the world (i.e. by the concepts typical of them) and by the new criteria of truth (or, if this is too narrow, the new criteria of what counts as rational belief) which go with them.

What then are the 'forms of knowledge'? I will not attempt an answer to this question by providing a list; instead, I will try to indicate the sorts of considerations relevant to answering it. To show, for example, that history was a separate form of knowledge would involve showing that historians possess and use peculiarly historical concepts and look for support for beliefs framed in terms of those concepts in ways which are distinctive of historical study. To do this, one would need a knowledge of history in the sense of being an active historian, rather than simply knowing some historical facts, and would have to stand back from the business of doing history in order to make an assessment of what was involved in it. In other words, one would have to engage in a second order activity in relation to the first order activity of doing history; that is, to become engaged in the philosophy of history.

Just as there is a philosophy of history, so too there is a philosophy of science, a philosophy of mathematics and so on; from which it is at least clear that there are fundamental differences between science, with its emphasis on observation and experimentation, and mathematics and logic, which do not seem to rely on anything like observation. It cannot, of course, be assumed, just because there is a philosophy of so-and-so, that therefore so-and-so has established its claim to the status of a separate form of knowledge, since the investigation of the claim to an independent status is one of the things with which its philosophy will be concerned. Whether, for example, there is a fundamental difference between the physical sciences and the social sciences, is one of the main topics in the philosophy of social science.

9 A BODY OF KNOWLEDGE

In a developed science such as physics many facts have been discovered about the physical nature of the world which, though they go beyond common sense and are available only to those who have studied the subject, are nevertheless so well supported that they are accepted as beyond dispute by everyone competent to form an opinion. They constitute a hard core of known facts. An example is Archimedes' principle that a floating body displaces its own weight in water.

Any student of the subject has to become acquainted with these facts, which constitute the established knowledge of the field of study. Only after this has been mastered can anyone hope to understand, let alone solve, the problems at the frontiers of the subject. Why, for example, does telepathy present a problem? Only because though it does seem to be a genuine phenomenon there is no known way in which it could occur. The transmission of something like electro-magnetic waves directly from one brain to another might be the answer; but all known forms of wave emission lose power with distance, whereas telepathic communication is independent of distance, and present knowledge of the structure of the brain suggests that it is not capable of acting as a transmitter in this way.

Though the facts which make up a body of knowledge are generally accepted as true, and further research in the subject is based on that assumption, they are not in principle beyond question. They are not in any sense absolutely true and may lose their status as truths altogether as a result of some radical theoretical revision, of the sort sometimes called a revolution. Some truths are more firmly entrenched than others, in the sense that if they are given up, many others go with them; but even the most firmly held truths are, in principle, subject to revision. Nevertheless, though such truths are not absolutely true, they go for the most part unquestioned; they can be accepted, with reasonable safety, as though they were absolutely true.

There is consequently a temptation for such subjects to be taught in ways which place emphasis primarily on the transmission of facts, with comparatively little attention being paid to the evidence for them. Even laboratory work and demonstrations may come to be valued on psychological grounds, as effective aids to teaching the facts, rather than as an integral part of the course. The techniques, methods and approach appropriate to research are then relegated to separate, independent courses, reserved for those whom they may concern. What is acquired by the student is true belief only, rather than rational belief. (There is of course an increasing realisation reflected, for example, in the Nuffield project, that some methods of teaching a subject, say physics, are more appropriate than others because they constitute an introduction to the method of enquiry employed by physicists, and do not simply acquaint the student with what has been established in physical science.)

For many purposes it is extremely useful to be acquainted with such a body of specialised, true beliefs about the world. It may, for example, be possible to arrive at true beliefs about future weather, relying on complex evidence interpreted in the light of modern research into the physics of the atmosphere. But what is important to the farmer with crops to harvest, or the family planning a picnic, is not the evidence on which the belief is based, but simply the truth about the weather.

On the other hand, somebody must be acquainted with the evidence if there are to be any grounds for saying that a belief is true at all. Moreover, anyone who values human rationality will wish to distinguish between equipping someone with information which will be useful in a limited context – though this may be an important part of his training for a particular job – and educating him.

10 THE USE OF DISCOVERY METHODS IN TEACHING MATHEMATICS

I mentioned, in the previous section, the possibility of teaching only the facts which constitute a body of established knowledge, with little attention to the evidence for them. I should like to develop this point by means of a discussion of the teaching of mathematics. In particular, I would like to discuss the demand that children should not merely learn to do sums, but should come to understand mathematics. What counts as understanding mathematics, as opposed to merely being able to do sums? According to the line of argument put forward in the previous section, what should be involved is that children should come to know, not just that four *is* the sum of two and two, but *why* four, and not five or six or three, is the correct answer. In other words, the aim would be to produce a rational belief that four is the sum of two and two (and, of course, a rational reliance on the calculations used in more complicated mathematical operations) and not merely a true belief that it is, or an ability to produce the right answer in more complicated cases. The grounds for advocating this approach are mathematical, therefore, not psychological.

It is not at all clear, however, that this is what is involved in the demand that mathematical understanding, and not just proficiency, be the aim. I propose, therefore, to look at the concept of understanding to try to understand what might be involved. I have previously discussed meaning; meaning attaches, primarily, to what people say. It is statements which people make which either have meaning, or fail to have meaning and are therefore nonsense. And just as what is said can also be heard, so what has meaning can also be understood. Any language (that is, any language which can be used to *say* anything) has a vocabulary as well as a grammar. The grammar, or syntax, governs the formulation of well-formed expressions in the language; the semantic rules relate what is said to the situations talked about when the sentence is used. And when we learn to talk, we learn by saying things and hearing things said. We don't first learn the syntax and only then add a vocabulary. By contrast with this, however, formal logical systems (with which I include mathematics) may be developed, and taught, in an uninterpreted form; no meaning is attached to the variables.

What then might be meant by saying that children should learn not merely to perform mathematical operations, but must also acquire understanding? Understanding cannot just be a psychological feeling which might be expressed by the words 'Ah, now I've got it', since people often feel they understand and express their feeling in this way when they have in fact failed to understand, and a warm glow of success is no substitute for success itself. What may be the case, however, is that children who have learnt their maths with 'understanding' in this sense are, as a matter of empirical fact, better placed to go on to more advanced maths than those who have learnt it in a different way. The new methods may bring no gain in the present (apart from the psychological feeling of confidence), but may pave the way for further mathematical progress in the future. But which methods are to be preferred for this reason can only be determined by long-term research and follow-up studies; it can't be inferred from the methods themselves.

All this, however, applies to mathematics taught as an uninterpreted system; but, of course, mathematics can be applied, or used, both in everyday life and in other subjects. Similarly, in the case of ordinary language we don't confine ourselves to constructing well-formed sentences like 'The king of France is wise' and leave it at that; normally, we construct the sentences in order to use them to say something. So in this sense children understand mathematics if they are not merely able to manipulate mathematical formulae, but are able to apply them to relevant situations; estimating the amount of wood needed for a job, for example. They learn not merely mathematics, but how to use mathematics.

Both of these aims – that children should learn mathematics in the early stages in such a way as to facilitate, rather than inhibit, future progress, and that they should learn not only mathematics but also how to make use of it – are eminently respectable. The only point I wish to make in the present connection is that neither of them is a demand for what I have called rational belief rather than mere true belief. Of course, a lot depends on just which methods are under discussion; I am thinking of things like Cuisenaire rods and Dienes blocks, and the use of the abacus, which have the effect of making the correct answer seem intuitively obvious. (My remarks do not, therefore, apply to revisions in the content of elementary mathematics courses, such as the inclusion of set theory, which allow the subject to be presented as a more coherent logical whole.) Such methods do not provide anything like a mathematical demonstration of the correctness of the answer. A child may learn that two and two equal four by physically adding two beads to two more and then counting up the total. It finds that there are four beads altogether and so becomes convinced of the truth of the mathematical proposition that two plus two equals four. But it would be a mistake to suppose that arithmetic was originally discovered by patiently counting little heaps of beads or of anything else. Mathematical truths are not generalisations from experience; their truth is independent of experience. And extensions to mathematical knowledge are not made in anything like this way; therefore, whatever the psychological advantages of employing such methods, they do not have the advantage of providing an introduction to the method whereby mathematical truths are established. Playing about with triangular pieces of board, and even measuring the angles, is no substitute for doing Euclid.

11 THE CURRICULUM

It would be absurd to suggest that in order to become educated it is necessary to learn everything that is known to man. Modern knowledge is too extensive for any one man to become familiar with more than a small part of it. Since specialisation is inevitable in the end, should it not therefore begin as early as possible? Or should the evil hour be delayed as long as possible?

Both of these are possible points of view, and both have their adherents. Early specialisation is favoured by those who take an instrumental view of education; the country needs scientists and technicians, and the primary task of education is to produce as many of them as possible as soon as possible as cheaply as possible. (It is obvious that there is no pressure on anyone to turn out low cost, mass produced philosophers.) It is this point of view which is reflected in the emphasis on the sort of examinations which provide public qualifications, useful in getting jobs and university places. And specialisation is also advocated (in favour of their own subject, but nevertheless more disinterestedly) by those who have come to think that the subject which they happen to teach is the only subject worth studying.

The opposite point of view, that men should at least be acquainted with all the possibilities of human knowledge, even if detailed knowledge is possible of only a small part of it, is more difficult to defend. But at least one argument for such an ideal follows from the account of education which I have offered. I took as my starting point the fact that education may be regarded as an activity which presents problems to those engaged in it. And, in the same way, human life as a whole is full of problems. Such problems come to us wearing no labels. There are no practical problems which are purely psychological; though of course there are theoretical problems which are purely psychological ones, i.e. those which psychologists as psychologists are concerned to answer. So, too, there are few problems to which moral considerations are not relevant, or considerations deriving from the scarcity of the means available to the attainment of our ends (i.e. economic considerations). Even the weight of people may be relevant in designing the gallery of a public hall. Suppose the problem is to decide on the size of classroom needed for thirty eight-year-old children. The specialist who has little idea even of the existence of alternative aspects of the problem will think that what he has to say is all there is to be said about the problem. The psychologist might talk about the effects of too large an area on group cohesion; the economist will count the cost; and so on. Relevant considerations will be adduced, but none of them will by itself provide a solution to the problem. And the danger is that the specialist may become arrogant through ignorance, thinking that what he has to say is all there is to say. But each of the developed forms of knowledge is the product of only a part of our experience. It is precisely because such viewpoints are partial that those whose knowledge concerns them are called specialists. And progress would, indeed, have come full circle if the part were substituted for the whole. Man would have become only a part of his former self; modern man would have become scientific man.

But even to argue this way is probably out of place. The preference for the 'rounded intellect' is probably most usually advocated simply as an educational ideal, as something desirable in itself irrespective of any further advantage to be obtained from it; the ideal that men, as men, should become acquainted with the full range of possibilities of experience which man's own endeavours have created.

12 KNOWING HOW AND KNOWING THAT

A distinction is often made, in connection with the concept of knowledge, between knowing how to do something and knowing that something is the case. This distinction is a reflection of the two possibilities opened up by the possession of a conceptual scheme: the possibility of belief and the possibility of action.

So far, I have related the concept of knowledge to the former – i.e. to the possibility of belief. Having distinguished between true belief and false belief, I drew attention to the use of the concept of knowledge to make explicit claims to rational belief. Such claims will be accepted by others who share, or who are brought to share, the same rational beliefs, and this is because a belief is rational in so far as it is based on evidence; and evidence is public, open to all, or at least to all who are competent in the particular field to which the belief belongs, if the belief is specialised.

How far can the concept of knowledge be extended to the practical possibilities opened up by the possession of a conceptual scheme? The position is complicated by the fact that the distinction, on which I have relied heavily, between a theoretical and a practical activity is not always easy to make. In the case of education I think the position is fairly clear; though even here the temptation to regard education as a theoretical activity rather than a practical one is reflected in the suggestion that theory of education represents an independent theoretical discipline. The status of morality and religion is even more ambiguous. Religion, for example, is, I think, best thought of as a practical rather than a theoretical activity. That is, it aims at a practical result rather than at the establishment of new truths. The practical result is something like: 'bringing the individual into a closer relationship with God'. But whatever the precise account of the practical result aimed at by religious practice (prayer, communal services, etc.) it is clear that it rests upon, or presupposes, at least one theoretical conclusion, i.e. that God exists. It is in an analogous way that education presupposes the possibility of knowledge. To be fully rational, those who engage in religious practice should be prepared to defend the truth of the premise on which their activity rests from sceptical attack; just as those who engage in the activity of education should be prepared to defend their presupposition from sceptical attack.

All this, however, represents no more than a complication, though an important one. The question I am now considering is whether it is proper to extend the concept of knowledge to the sphere of practical activities like religion and morality. I think it proper to do so in so far as behaviour, as well as belief, may be subject to assessment. Beliefs are subject to assessment primarily by reference to evidence. The criteria for the assessment of behaviour will be different, but may nevertheless exist. Actions done in order to bring about a certain result may be assessed for their efficiency; are they in fact likely to bring about the intended result? And is the manner in which the result is to be achieved acceptable? I may satisfy my hunger by catching the cat and taking a bite out of it, but would lay myself open to reproach if not indigestion. And, more important still, are the ends towards which I direct efforts the ends I ought to have? I spend my time, perhaps, studying philosophy; ought I not to spend it instead sporting with Amaryllis in the shade?

Fortunately, I do not have to pursue these difficult questions further; since they, together with the rest of the problems of ethics, will be the subject of a separate volume in this series.

SUMMARY

1. The analyses offered of educational concepts are based primarily on our ordinary use of language, but also recommend an amended or more precise use of language.

2. An understanding of the concept of knowledge will be more easily achieved if the use of 'I know' (i.e. the verb to know) is considered before going on to consider the substantive 'knowledge'.

3. We use the words 'I know' to claim that a particular belief which we hold is a rational belief. Ayer's account of knowledge was considered.

4. Ayer's requirement that what is known must be true leads to scepticism if interpreted as a condition which must be satisfied in addition to the requirement that what is known must be based on evidence.

5. Claims to know are in principle always open to challenge. The question 'Do you really know?' does not lead to scepticism, provided it is interpreted as meaning 'Do you have good evidence for your belief?' rather than 'Is what you take to be true on the best available evidence really true?' The possibility of knowledge is presupposed in education; if the sceptic's version of the question is admitted, therefore, it must be answered.

6. In practice, there are many facts which are accepted without question, since the evidence for them is freely available to all. The more sophisticated beliefs are possible only for those who possess the necessary conceptual apparatus, and rational belief is possible only for those who are acquainted with the specialised procedures for establishing truth in that particular field.

7. Specialised conceptions of the world develop out of the shared, common sense conception of the world of a particular society, bringing with them new possibilities of belief and new criteria of truth.

8. Forms of knowledge are distinguished from one another by the concepts and criteria of truth peculiar to them.

9. In a developed subject there are many facts which, though not in principle beyond challenge, are well established and very generally accepted. The teaching of such a subject may come to concentrate on the transmission of these facts, neglecting the evidence for them.

10. Mathematical truths are not established empirically; the use of discovery methods, therefore, has only a psychological justification, not a mathematical one.

11. A broadly-based curriculum will provide an introduction into all the main forms of knowledge. Those who then proceed to acquire more detailed specialised knowledge will not then suppose that what they have to say on any practical problem is all there is to be said.

12. Standards may be applied to practices as well as beliefs; the concept of knowledge has application, therefore, to practical as well as theoretical activities.

FURTHER READING

1. On ordinary language, and the difficulties involved in relying on it, see Chappell (27), and especially Austin's 'A Plea for Excuses'. On philosophical arguments generally, see Passmore (66).

2. For Moore's views on 'good' see Moore (57, chapter 1) and for Hare's see Hare (41, Part Two). Austin discusses the question 'how do you know?' and the use of 'I know' in Flew (33, chapter 8).

3. For Ayer's discussion of knowledge see Ayer (10). The account of knowledge discussed is in chapter 1, section 5. Ayer takes scepticism about the possibility of knowledge seriously, and much of his book is taken up with showing that knowledge is nevertheless possible. On knowledge and belief generally, see Woozley (109, chapter 8), Chisholm (28) and Scheffler (86). Ackermann (2) provides selections from classical sources accompanied by critical commentary. On John Locke see Aaron (1) and O'Connor (62).

4. See Austin's discussion (6) of doubts about whether we ever 'really' see material objects like tables and chairs, especially his discussion of 'real' and 'really' in chapter 7.

5. On facts, see Lucas (116).

6. Hanson (40, especially chapter 1 (observation) and chapter 2 (facts)), discusses the sense in which observation, particularly in science, is 'theory-laden'; asking, for example, whether a trained

physicist and an Eskimo baby would see the same thing when looking at an X-ray tube.

8. On forms of knowledge, see Hirst (chapter 5 in 4). On the philosophy of history, see Dray (30), Walsh (101) and Gardiner (34). On the philosophy of science, see Toulmin (97), Harré (42), Pap (64) and Braithwaite (23).

On the philosophy of the social sciences, see Braybrooke (24) and Gibson (36).

10. My remarks in this section are not intended to be critical of attempts being made, especially in primary schools, to put the teaching of mathematics on a more satisfactory basis. It may well be that the scope, and indeed the need, for rational belief in mathematics is limited. For the majority of children what is important is not that their knowledge should be placed on a fully rational basis, but that they should be able to make practical use of what knowledge they have. An experimental psychologist may quite properly rely on statistical techniques which are known to be reliable (known, that is, by statisticians) without himself knowing why they are reliable.

Contrary to what I stated in the text, John Stuart Mill held the view that mathematical truths are generalisations, of the most general sort, from experience; see Mill (54, Book II, chapter 6, paragraphs one and two). On the philosophy of mathematics, see Barker (13).

The connection between 'understanding' and 'meaning' can be brought out by considering what is involved in saying that a child understands what it reads. In one sense a child can read if it can reproduce verbally what is presented in printed form on the page, but it can achieve this translation without understanding. The spoken words have the same meaning as the printed words, but the child understands the meaning of neither. Or a child may understand part of what the writer meant; it may interpret Shakespeare literally, but not take the full meaning. Whether understanding has been achieved depends, as with learning, on the standard adopted; on what we are prepared to accept as counting as understanding. Cf. chapter 3, section 5 (pages 41–3) and chapter 8, section 5 (pages 121–4).

11. Scheffler (86) discusses the impossibility of any one person becoming acquainted with the whole of modern knowledge in connection with his discussion of philosophy as a super-science.

Hirst (chapter 5 in 4) presents a convincing case for liberal education as intended to provide at least acquaintance with all the possibilities of knowledge.

12. A sharp distinction between knowing how and knowing that is made by Ryle (83, chapter 2).

8 Teaching

I TEACHERS AND TEACHING

I suggested that education in the formal sense begins when one person consciously accepts responsibility for the learning of another. Much of what has to be learnt by the child in order to become educated is learnt without such help; for example, learning to talk. By contrast, there are many things which few children acquire without special help, for example, mathematics or physics or Latin. We use the word 'teachers' to refer to those who go out of their way to provide such help; and the word 'teaching' to refer to what they do in providing it.

It does not follow, however, that the notion of teaching is properly applied only to the transmission of what I have called 'formal knowledge' of curriculum subjects. It is true, for example, that most children learn to talk without anyone teaching them to do so; but some do not. And if a child fails to learn to talk without help it is important – that is educationally important – that help be provided. There is, of course, a problem about what form that help should take: the teacher may be able to do no more than most parents do automatically; that is, place the child in an environment containing other human beings who talk to each other and to the child about the things in the immediate environment. But the question of how to go about teaching a child to talk is a psychological one, about which too little is known. My point is simply that teaching a child to talk is a proper educational concern because language is an essential part of all human activities. And the argument could be repeated for learning to walk, to manipulate objects and pick things up. Here, failure to learn without special help would presumably be due to physical rather than mental handicap. But whatever the cause of

H

failure, it presents an educational problem because of the importance of mobility in normal human life.

Of course, not everything which is learnt, with or without help, is part of becoming educated. The use of the term 'education' implies that what is learnt is regarded as being of value. In the case of informal education, the person committed to the value judgement is the person who thinks the term 'education' applies. In the case of formal education, the person who accepts responsibility for seeing that learning occurs is also responsible for the content of that learning; he is committed, that is, to the value judgement that what he passes on is worth passing on. A teacher who passes on certain beliefs about the physical world is committed, as a teacher, to passing on only those beliefs which he himself accepts as true. If he passes on views about how other people should be treated, he will pass on only those views which he himself accepts as morally right.

I need, then, to give an account of what teaching is; and this I propose to do in this chapter. What is not so obvious is that a separate account is needed of what a teacher is; for a teacher is one who teaches, and given that we know what teaching is, what more is there to say? But teaching often takes place in socially structured situations – that is in schools – distinguished by the presence of both teachers and pupils, and I do not think that an understanding of 'teaching' is by itself sufficient to give us an understanding of such situations. In the following chapter, therefore, I will go on to make some remarks about the pupil-teacher relationship.

2 TEACHING AS AN ACTIVITY

Teaching occurs when one person consciously accepts responsibility for the learning of another. And, subject to certain qualifications, we use the word 'teaching' to refer to what they do in order to bring about that learning.

It is, therefore, at least obvious that teaching is doing something. But is this to say anything at all? I shall try to show that it is by offering an answer to the question 'What is it to do something?', i.e. 'What is it to perform a (human) action?'

Examples of actions, of people doing things, are easy to find; so easy, in fact, that it is not obvious that there is any problem here. 'Chopping wood', 'reading a newspaper' and 'teaching' are all perfectly good answers to the question 'What are you doing?' But it does not follow that an easy answer is available to the question, 'What, in general, is it to do something?' What is wanted here is an elucidation of the concept of a human action, and this is far from easy to provide. I will try to draw attention to some of the problems, referring, by way of illustration, to the adventures of Humpty Dumpty. Humpty Dumpty sat on a wall; and that was something which he did. But he also fell off the wall; and having a great fall was not something which he did; rather it was something which happened to him. So all the events in a person's life are not things that he does; some of them are things which happen to him. Again examples are easy to find: slipping on banana skins, going berserk, and being born, are all things that happen to people; not to mention becoming conditioned, being hypnotised and getting seduced. But, again, what in general is the difference between someone's doing something, and something happening to them?

Actions often form part of some more or less elaborate plan, or pattern of activity, in which a person is engaged; this is certainly true of gardening or teaching. So at least one can make the negative point that falling off the wall was not part of any plan which Humpty Dumpty was engaged in carrying out. Sitting on the castle wall was part of some plan of his; or, if 'plan' is too pretentious a word here, sitting on the wall was his idea of how to spend Sunday morning; whereas cracking his shell on the pavement was not.

But what made it possible for Humpty Dumpty to set out to sit on the wall, in a way in which he did not set out to fall off? In sitting on the wall, he was aware of what he was doing, in the sense that he knew what a wall was, and what it would be like for him to sit on it, just as he might have known what it would have been like for the cat to sit on the mat or the dish to run away with the spoon. More generally, he had some conception of the world and of himself as part of it. And this made it possible for him to suppose, when he was not on the wall, that he might be on it; to consider sitting on the wall as something he might do. It need not be supposed that he ever said to himself, 'What should I do this morning?', replying 'I know, I'll sit on the castle wall'; though he may have done so. But in so far as sitting on the wall is something he did, it will make sense to say that it is something which he chose to do. There are some things which someone could not choose to do because he could not conceive of the possibility of doing them. A child, for example, could not decide to form a limited liability company, not only because of his legal disability, but because it does not know what a limited liability company is. Falling off the wall is something Humpty Dumpty *might* have chosen to do; though the circumstantial evidence is against its being something he actually did. He had no reason to throw himself off, as people sometimes do have a reason for throwing themselves off the Empire State Building.

In the same way, when the teachers return to school on Monday morning, at least we know that they are not there because the wind was blowing in that direction. And so on throughout the teaching day; in so far as they are teaching, and to teach is to do something, they are in the position of Humpty Dumpty on the wall rather than Humpty Dumpty on the floor. They don't, of course, have a privileged immunity from things happening to them between the hours of nine and four; on the contrary. Everything that happens to a person is not attributable to the impersonal forces of nature like the wind and the force of gravity, and 'don't turn your back' is sound advice in many teaching situations.

3 TEACHING AS GOAL-DIRECTED

Humpty Dumpty was sitting on the wall because he wanted to; it was just one of the things he liked to do. But many of the things we do are done with some further end in mind, something which is not directly involved in the action itself. In addition to the question 'what are you doing?', a further question is often appropriate: 'why are you doing it?' Sometimes, indeed, the action is unintelligible to us unless this further question is answered. If, for example, someone is sitting on the top of a thirty-foot pole in the middle of the desert, then his action itself is unintelligible to us unless we know why he is doing it; unless, that is, his action is placed in a context of human wants and activities. Answers like 'to win the world-pole-sitter-onner championship' or 'to bring me nearer to the Great Spirit' bring at least partial understanding. On the other hand, the answer 'because I want to' would not; normal people don't 'just want' that sort of thing.

There are many actions performed in the course of teaching which taken in isolation are trivial even if not unintelligible. Is sharpening pencils, for example, to count as teaching? If they are being sharpened just for the pleasure of it, like whittling a stick, that is in itself intelligible, but what is being done cannot count as teaching. For that, the action must be done with a further purpose in mind and, moreover, a particular purpose. In order to accept sharpening pencils as a teaching activity, we need to know why they are being sharpened, to see that particular action as fitting into a pattern of actions and to see how the pattern of actions is expected to help someone to learn something. Teaching is not just goal-directed, but directed towards a particular goal: the bringing about of learning.

The connection between 'teaching 'and 'learning' is conceptual; that is, it is a connection between the concepts 'teaching' and 'learning'. To understand what teaching is, you need to understand that it is an activity consciously undertaken in order that somebody should learn something. And to say this is not to deny that people do teach for all sorts of reasons; to earn a living, or because they like children and so on. But these are empirical facts which do not help us to understand what teaching is.

Any activity which aims at a particular result runs the risk of failing to achieve that result, and teaching is no exception. It may be undertaken with or without success. In terms of the distinction made earlier, 'teaching' is a task word, not an achievement word; teaching is more like running a race than winning a race. We don't, as a matter of fact, have a separate word for 'teaching successfully', comparable to 'winning a race' instead of 'running in a race successfully'. So we do tend to use the same word 'teaching' when talking about the outcome as well as the attempt, and this can lead to misunderstanding. When we do attribute success we have to rely on the context to make this clear, as in 'I taught myself French in six months'; or make an explicit reference to success, as in 'He succeeded in teaching the natives to feel guilty'.

But since the attempt, if not the achievement, is essential to teaching, it is important to be clear about what is going to count as success.

4 SUCCESS IN TEACHING

Anyone who aims at a particular result must, at least, have a clear idea of what that result is. The discussion of 'aiming' earlier on is relevant here. If a man is aiming at something, then even though he misses the target he must know what he is aiming at. If he doesn't know that, then he can't (logically) be successful, no matter what he hits. An arrow fired at random will no doubt fall somewhere; it may end up sticking out of a partridge or a poacher. But the archer cannot claim to have been successful in hitting anything, because he didn't set out to hit anything.

In one sense, the aim in teaching is always the same, to bring about learning. But this is no more helpful in practice than saying that archers always aim at targets. Just as on each occasion a particular target must be aimed at, so too learning must always take a particular form. So if anything is to count as success in teaching, the teacher must have a fairly precise idea of what he hopes will be learnt.

An important part of the professional training of a teacher consists in acquiring such an idea. Above the primary level, teachers tend to specialise in teaching particular subjects, geography, history and so on, and the studies of their pupils are ordered by a curriculum based on the established disciplines. The geography teacher, for example, needs to know some geography himself, and what he tries to do in teaching is to help his pupils to learn some geography.

This seems so obvious as to be scarcely worth saying. But below the secondary level, and especially in the infants' and nursery schools, the matter is not so obvious. What is the difference between a nursery school and a day nursery? Nursery schools are educational institutions, and are staffed by qualified nursery

teachers; whereas day nurseries simply look after children while
their mothers are at work. But these answers are very little help.
What is the difference, at this level, between teaching children and
simply looking after them? What is a nursery teacher qualified
by her training to do?

These questions cannot be answered simply by looking at
what goes on in nursery schools and comparing it with what
goes on in day nurseries. Both may provide much the same facilities for the children in their charge: a garden to play in and a tree
to climb on, a sand-pit and a large bath of water, and so on. The
important difference lies elsewhere, in the intention with which
these facilities are provided. In the day nursery the intention is
to keep the children amused and out of mischief until their
mothers collect them. In the nursery school the aim is different;
it is to bring about learning, to foster the intellectual and social
development of the children. The provision of opportunities to
play with sand and water or with coloured beads and counting
frames, or of clothes to dress up in, or empty boxes to make
models with, can all count as teaching methods; provided, that is,
the teachers who provide such opportunities have a clear idea of
what they hope to achieve by using them.

Why is it important to insist on this? Isn't it good enough that
teachers should be trained in the right methods? The right methods are those which produce the right results, so somebody
must know what counts as the right results. But need the teacher
herself know? Can't she leave it to her mentors to say which
methods are the right ones? To revert to the travel metaphor
discussed earlier, are not detailed instructions on how to proceed
good enough? This is certainly a possible way to carry on, though
if what I have said about 'teaching' is correct it would not be
teaching. But does it matter what it is called, so long as the result
is the same?

Earlier I argued that rational belief was preferable to true
belief on the grounds that beliefs which are held because of the
evidence for them can be revised in the light of fresh evidence or
after fresh consideration of the existing evidence. Similar considerations apply here. Unless the teacher has a clear idea what is
to be learnt, she (or he) will not be in a position to judge for

herself whether a particular method is likely to be successful in bringing learning about, nor can her efforts be intelligently adapted to changing circumstances and particular cases so as to make success more likely. It is true that it is difficult to form a clear idea of what the child needs to learn at this stage; it can't be set out neatly like the syllabus for O-level maths. I have tried, in my remarks on informal education, to give some idea of what is involved. My remarks there might be summed up by saying that what the teacher tries to do is change his or her pupils' conception of themselves and of the world they live in; and to do this, primarily, by introducing them to a language which reflects the shared, public conception of the world of the society in which they live.

Given a clear conception of what it is that has to be learnt, it will then be possible to compare teaching methods in respect of their tendency to produce the desired result, i.e. to assess their relative efficiency. This will be done partly by the individual teacher on the basis of personal experience, and more systematically by means of psychological research. Detailed studies may be made, for example, of the relative effectiveness of different methods of teaching reading to children suffering from a variety of disabilities, or of using the Initial Teaching Alphabet as compared with the normal one in teaching normal children to read and write. And psychology will also be relevant in suggesting, on general theoretical grounds such as those provided by learning theory, that certain methods are likely to be more efficient than others. Considerations of this sort may lead, for example, to a preference for methods in which the material to be learnt is always presented in such a way as to preclude the possibility of a mistake, so ensuring that every step which is taken by the learner is a step in the right direction; or for methods which allow the learner to find the correct answer by a process of exploration, learning by his mistakes.

Equally important to success in teaching will be knowledge of the development of children, especially young children. The teacher needs to know what it is reasonable to expect from children of different ages, as well as the extent to which children of the same age differ in their ability, and also to be aware of their emotional needs and problems. But though the teacher will naturally look to the developmental psychologist for knowledge of the needs of young children, it is important to note the limitations on the psychologists' qualifications to give this. For statements of what children (or anyone else) need are not simply statements of psychological fact. This is because the concept of need is a complex one, which allows us to conflate a judgement about what is the case with a value judgement. Tiggy needs a woman, a stable boy may say; no, Teapot may reply, Tiggy *wants* a woman, but what Tiggy needs is a dose of salts. They are in agreement about Tiggy's psychological condition; what they disagree about is what should be done about it. And statements that children need love and affection are logically similar. The psychologist's point is that lack of love now will not only cause them suffering now, but will harm them in the future as well. And, of course, this is an important discovery. But the point is that what counts as *harm* is not the result of a psychological discovery; it is a reflection of what we value in human life. Statements about children's need for love take such valuations for granted; as indeed they are quite entitled to do. In the context of a shared morality no one is likely to be led astray. But it is worth pointing out that such valuations are not founded on psychological evidence nor could they be so founded. The psychologist is not an expert in making moral judgements, any more than the philosopher is. The position is rather that we are all experts; which is as much as to say that there are no experts.

5 THE CRITERIA OF SUCCESS

Success in teaching consists in the bringing about of learning; but how do we establish whether learning has taken place? It will certainly not be possible to do so without first giving some clear indication of what it is that is required to have been learnt. In the case of young children it is difficult to do this with any precision, for reasons which I gave in the preceding section; and it will be equally difficult to provide clear-cut criteria of success. And, in practice, one may be driven back to consideration of methods used, and call teaching competent, if not successful, if it relies on methods which in general are likely to produce the required learning. For this reason it is especially important for teachers of young children to be acquainted with what research findings exist on the relative efficiency of different teaching methods. Because of the difficulty of established criteria of success for the sort of learning which young children are required to achieve, I will confine my discussion in this section to what should be the easier case, successful learning of curriculum studies.

I suggested earlier that 'learning' is best used in a way which is neutral as to the way in which learning occurs, but which refers to the fact that a change in belief or behaviour is to count as a success or achievement. In the same way, I think 'teaching' is best used to refer to the help provided by teachers in their efforts to bring about learning, whatever form that help takes; it is not, that is, to be identified with the adoption of any particular method. A child, for example, arrives breathless and eager for a geography lesson, and goes on its way rejoicing half an hour later. Has it learnt anything in the intervening time? To answer this question, it is no use asking what went on during the lesson. The teacher, aware perhaps that it is better to succeed in jumping over a mole hill than to fall flat on your back trying to jump over the moon, decided to attempt to put over one simple fact; that Paris is the capital of France. In order to achieve this he may have told the class that Paris is the capital of France. He may have had them write it down or recite it in unison. Or he may have appealed to their interests, and told them a long involved story about a man who went to *Paris* and met a girl called Fifi la Bonne Bonne who was *French*. But he won't have succeeded in teaching them anything unless they know that Paris is the capital of France at the end of the lesson and did not know it at the beginning. Teaching is successful if learning has occurred; but whether learning has occurred is itself only to be decided by the application of the relevant criteria of success.

What the relevant criteria of success are is internal to the matter to be learnt; they are not to be decided arbitrarily, as in the case of the pigeon trained to walk with its head in the air, but are supplied impersonally by the relevant discipline. Thus, in learning arithmetic success consists, in the most modest case, in being able to provide the answer 'four' as the sum of two and two. 'Five' just won't do, any more than 'Rome' is acceptable as the answer to the question 'What is the capital of France?' It is true that in the classroom what the teacher says goes; it is the teacher who puts the ticks and crosses in the exercise book. But the teacher is not free to put them where he feels like putting them; he, in turn, is governed by impersonal criteria of success. To fail to realise this, and therefore to regard the marks given as a reflection of the teacher's attitude to the student personally rather than to his work, is not only to fail to learn any arithmetic (or whatever the subject is) but to fail also to realise that arithmetic is an activity in which *something* counts as success.

But though the sort of thing which counts as success is laid down by the relevant discipline, this still leaves room for differences in standards. There is, therefore, an arbitrary element in the assessment of learning; in the sense that the actual standard adopted is not determined by the subject. All the correct moves may be made towards the solution of a problem in arithmetic, but due to a small slip at the last stage the final answer is wrong. Are no marks to be given, or nine out of ten? Does an examinee get no marks for the knowledge he shows of his subject, even though it is strictly irrelevant to the question as set? Are marks to be awarded for style in an answer to a history question, or for historical knowledge in an English essay? The point is not that two people may disagree about the correct answer to a question, though of course they may do; especially as the well-trodden paths of established knowledge are left behind for the 'frontiers of knowledge'. But two people who are in substantial agreement about the answer to a question may still adopt different standards; as indeed may the same person on different occasions, without in any way changing his views about the subject matter concerned.

Of course, the actual standard adopted will be arbitrary only in the sense that it is not determined by the subject matter; but it will be related to the purpose for which the measurement is made. Measurements in education are commonly made for purposes of comparison; to see who has learnt best, or is likely to learn best, rather than simply to see what learning has taken place. If all the candidates get full marks, or all get no marks, this will not allow any comparison to be made. On the other hand, the wider the base of comparison the more information is conveyed by the mark given. So the standard chosen will be one which will give a good spread of marks, allowing every candidate to be placed relative to the rest; and, ideally, 'the rest' will include not only other students in the same year, but those who took the examination in previous years also.

Whether we say that learning has taken place is, therefore, to some extent an artifact of the scoring system, and to the extent that this is so, success in teaching is also dependent on the scoring system adopted. Ideally at least, the person who has done the teaching is the person best qualified to choose the scoring system. He is the one who has been trying to bring learning about, and he knows what he hoped would be learnt; he also knows the individual and collective capacity of his class better than anyone else. Public examinations have their uses, especially in broadening the basis of comparison made by the marks given, but their use to assess *teachers* is appropriate only if it is accepted that the teacher's whole task is laid down for him by a statement of examination requirements of a remote and impersonal board. The alternative is to accept that teachers do lay down their own standards, at least in important respects, and that the only real guarantee of the successful performance of their job lies in their own professional training and integrity.

6 TEACHING AND RATIONALITY

I have argued that 'teaching' is not the name of a method of doing anything, any more than 'learning' is the name of any process. The teacher must do something if he is to be instrumental in helping anyone to learn; he must rely on some method, just as there must be some way in which learning occurs. But reliance on no particular method is dictated by the meaning of 'teaching'.

Nevertheless, moral restrictions on what is an acceptable teaching method do follow from the meaning of 'teaching'. But before going on to consider these in detail. I want to consider a suggestion made by Professor Scheffler that teaching is distinguished by 'its special connection with rational explanation and critical dialogue'.

As far as I understand his account, he seems to be suggesting that the use of rational methods follows from the meaning of 'teaching', and that 'teaching' is the name of a method of inducing belief. Teaching, threats, force, etc., have in common the fact that they are methods of inducing belief; what differentiates teaching is its connection with rationality. Scheffler does not actually say that 'teaching' is the name of a method of producing belief; but I think this follows from what he does say. He says that 'one may try to propagate a belief in numerous ways other than teaching – for example, through deception, insinuation, advertising, hypnosis, propaganda, indoctrination, threats, bribery, and force'. And he goes on to point out that 'formal agencies of schooling . . . often employ methods other than teaching'. 'What distinguishes teaching is its special connection with rational explanation and critical dialogue: with the enterprise of giving honest reasons and welcoming radical questions. The person engaged in teaching does not merely want to bring about belief, but to bring it about through the exercise of free rational judgement by the student. This is what distinguishes teaching from propaganda or debating, for example. In teaching, the teacher is revealing his reasons for the beliefs he wants to transmit and is thus, in effect, submitting his own judgement to the critical scrutiny and evaluation of the student; he is fully engaged in the dialogue by which he hopes to teach, and is thus risking his own beliefs, in lesser or greater degree, as he teaches. Teaching . . . involves trying to bring about learning under severe restrictions of manner – that is to say, within the limitations imposed by the framework of rational discussion.'

While I share Scheffler's preference for rationality, I think it should be made clear that this is a preference which requires justification. I think it is better, therefore, not to write it into either the concept of education or the concept of teaching. I have already given some indication of the lines which such a defence might take. My present concern is to reject the suggestion that 'teaching' is the name of any method of bringing about learning and is, therefore, not the name of the rational methods of producing beliefs which Scheffler describes.

If the connection between teaching and rationality is as close as Scheffler suggests, a great deal of what we normally call teaching is ruled out. It is quite unrealistic to suppose that teachers in nursery and infants' schools spend more than a tiny fraction of their time doing anything like giving rational explanations or engaging in critical dialogue. In so far as they share Scheffler's preference for rationality, they will offer rational explanations whenever they think there is any point in doing so. Most of the time there isn't; but teachers in such schools still think they put in a full day's teaching. Most of the methods on which they rely are indirect and informal and the results, to the casual observer, chaotic or at least haphazard. But they count as teaching methods because of the intention with which they are used; they are chosen as teaching methods because they are considered likely to bring about the required learning. The choice of methods may be criticised as mistaken (though more thought has been given to the choice of method at this level of education than at any other); but it would be quite unjustifiable to rule out, on purely logical grounds, methods which have been adopted after careful consideration and in the belief that they will bring about the sort of learning appropriate to that educational level.

Even at the level of education which fits Scheffler's case best, it is misleading to say that 'in so far as the teacher is teaching, he is ... risking his own particular truth judgements, for he is exposing them to the general critique of [the relevant criteria] and to the free critical judgement of the student's mind'. Most of what is taught, even in universities, and almost all of what is taught in schools, belongs to what I have called established knowledge. It would take more than a few off-the-cuff remarks from a student to shake a physics teacher's acceptance of the second law of thermodynamics or of Archimedes' principle. Of course, in a subject like philosophy there is very little which does count as established knowledge. Even in philosophy, however, there are standard criticisms of certain philosophical positions and, in practice, a first-year student who rejects these has almost certainly failed to see the point of them. Moreover, the most important part of what the student has to learn is how to be critical in a particular field, rather than a set of beliefs, however acquired. And, once he is really in a position to criticise the teacher's 'own particular truth judgements', the main part of the teaching job is over; it becomes a moot point who is teaching who.

But if teaching is not to be distinguished from 'deception, insinuation, advertising, hypnosis, propaganda, indoctrination, threats, bribery and force' by the methods on which it relies, how is the contrast to be made? Some of the items on the list can be eliminated because they *are* the names of methods of doing something, i.e. deception, insinuation, hypnosis, threats, bribery and force, and conditioning might be added to the list. But advertising, propaganda and indoctrination are not the names of methods of doing anything, any more than teaching is. What is distinctive of them is not the methods on which they rely, but what they aim at. Advertising is concerned to increase the demand for particular products, propaganda to produce or maintain a positive attitude to a particular government, and indoctrination to obtain acceptance of certain beliefs; just as teaching aims at bringing about learning. But nothing is laid down by the meaning of the words 'advertising', 'propaganda', 'indoctrination' or 'teaching' about the precise methods to be adopted, though, since the methods chosen will be those thought likely to produce the required results, some methods will be typical of each.

I have already indicated that there are moral restrictions on what is acceptable as a teaching method implicit in the meaning of 'teaching'. 'Advertising', 'indoctrination' and 'propaganda' do not have the same moral restrictions built in. Advertising men at least claim that their profession has a professional ethic to go with it. 'Indoctrination' seems to have a sort of studied indifference written in, so far as the morality of the means to be adopted is concerned. What is held to be morally important, in indoctrination, is that certain beliefs should become accepted; concern for the propagation of the right doctrine dwarfs all other considerations. And the term 'propaganda' has come to imply positive licence as far as the morality of the means is concerned; nor is it required that the beliefs being transmitted should be accepted as true by those responsible for their transmission.

In the case of 'teaching', it certainly does follow from the meaning of the word that in passing on beliefs about the world, the teacher is passing on those beliefs which he himself accepts as true. The teacher is trying to bring about learning, and no one has learnt anything if he has come to accept a belief which is not true. If you have learnt something when you come to believe that Guinness is good for you, you have done so only because Guinness *is* good for you. And if a belief is true, it will be possible (at least in principle) to produce evidence for it; production of evidence will, therefore, be a method of producing belief which is open to the teacher. And if what he is trying to do is produce rational belief rather than merely true belief, this will be the only way he can proceed.

The concern with truth is less close in the case of indoctrination. The beliefs put forward for acceptance are also accepted as true beliefs by those putting them forward, but they are offered for uncritical acceptance only, and are probably held uncritically by those putting them forward. The beliefs which are the subject of indoctrination are, in fact, usually held as absolutely true, in a way which makes criticism of them not merely unnecessary, but sacrilegious or heretical.

Advertisers, I suppose, like to think that the claims they make on behalf of their clients are true, but more, perhaps, because they will otherwise fail to carry conviction rather than out of any regard for truth as such. Their homage is reserved, not for the word, but for the dollar; they are not so much mistaken as unprincipled. And propaganda is often concerned deliberately to distort the truth, since no sane person in possession of the facts could possibly behave in the way in which governments sometimes expect their subjects to behave. Only by acquiring the most warped view of the facts could anyone be brought to drop napalm bombs on children or take part in the systematic liquidation of a race.

I have, then, distinguished advertising, propaganda and indoctrination from teaching in terms of their purposes, by the extent to which moral restrictions are placed on the ways in which those purposes may be achieved, and by reference to the commitment involved to the truth of the beliefs to be produced.

The last two criteria are related. Since the belief being transmitted in advertising, propaganda or indoctrination may be false, or at least accepted as true uncritically, it will not be possible to get anyone to believe it by presenting the evidence for it, since there won't be any evidence, or, at least, any adequate evidence, to support it. So in these cases you either have to go through a parody of producing evidence or rely on some other method altogether. The choice is between dishonesty – accepting the fact that the person to acquire the belief is a rational creature capable of basing his beliefs on the evidence for them, but tricking him by cooking the evidence; or the grosser form of immorality in which others are manipulated without regard for their humanity, and treated like animals in the farmyard.

Advertising is, perhaps, the least pernicious of the three. Many of the claims made by advertisers are true and they do a useful job in informing the consumer of the goods available for purchase. A great deal of advertising is simply persuasion, but involves no deception, since it is easily recognisable for what it is. Nobody, for example, really expects the girl in the bikini to be delivered with the car, though they may be persuaded by the picture to buy the car.

It is the sort of advertising which goes through a parody of producing the evidence for a belief which is false which seems to me to be most dishonest. I will offer an example, therefore, of what I mean by 'going through a parody of producing the evidence'. Sales of margarine have to compete with those of butter, since margarine and butter are close substitutes for each other. And many people choose to buy butter, even though margarine is cheaper and keeps better and is just as nutritious, because they say they prefer the taste. But if it could be shown that they couldn't really tell the difference between butter and margarine, their reason for choosing butter would be discredited, and their preference for it shown to rest on prejudice.

There are, in fact, well-established ways of deciding questions of this sort; psychologists have conducted extensive research into people's powers of sensory discrimination and have developed techniques for doing so. No sophisticated technique is required to show that people of normal eyesight can discriminate between, say, two lights which differ greatly in intensity, say a candle and a searchlight. But if the difference in intensity is progressively reduced, it does become difficult and eventually impossible to discriminate between the two light sources. But no one claims that the difference between margarine and butter is as great as the difference between a candle and a searchlight; if it were, they would not compete for the same market, for they would not be close substitutes for one another. So the margarine–butter case is more like the two lights which don't differ very much in brightness, rather than the candle–searchlight case.

To establish whether there is a discriminable difference between the brightness of two light sources, or the taste of two things, you need to take a number of subjects and give them each a number of tests. Each test consists simply in asking them to say which of two light sources is brighter or which of two samples is margarine. You need to test a number of people, because people vary in their powers of discrimination, and you need to test each person more than once because, for reasons connected with the properties of the central nervous system, the same person's powers of discrimination vary slightly from one moment to another. But now what counts as being able to tell the difference? If you get only five trials out of six right, then you got one wrong, so on at least one occasion you couldn't tell the difference. If you really couldn't tell the difference if, that is, you were just guessing, you should get three out of six right, since you have a fifty-fifty chance on each trial anyway. But if you get four out of six, you have done better than chance. And if the average score of a large number of people is four out of six, this is just the sort of evidence for saying that there is a discriminable difference between butter and margarine. If only one person in six scores six out of six, this will show only that the difference between the brightness of the lights or the taste of the two things is not perfectly obvious; which no one claimed anyway. If we have no information about the scores of those who did not get six out of six, we do not have sufficient evidence to enable us to decide whether most people (i.e. more than half) can or cannot tell the difference. But if one person in six does score six out of six, this strongly suggests that most people can make the required discrimination. For if one person in six scores six out of six, it is extremely improbable that the other five will have averaged only two point four, which they would have to have done for the overall average score to be no better than chance, i.e. three out of six.

Moral restrictions on what is acceptable as a teaching method spring from the nature of the activity of teaching in two ways.

In the first place, the teaching situation necessarily involves interaction between human beings and it is intrinsic to such interactions that they are governed by moral considerations. And the teacher, in accepting responsibility for the learning of another, is not thereby released from the normal restraints which moral rules impose on conduct. To say that someone is a teacher is not to deny that he is subject to moral rules; as to say that someone was a member of the state police (or a Hobbesian sovereign) might be to say that he is above the law. Nor is it to say that he is someone who is known to be immoral, like a murderer or a prostitute or a libertine. The teacher owes to his pupils the same basic respect which is due to any human being; nor does it follow from the fact that he is a teacher that he has failed or is likely to fail to accord to others the moral respect due to them. The fact that the pupils are children, as is often the case, is important, but no more so than in any situation in which children are involved. A motorist should take special care when driving past a school about the hour when the children are coming out, but that does not mean that there is some special connection between being a motorist and children. Motorists have a moral responsibility to take reasonable care not to knock anyone down; special care when driving past a school is needed simply because children are less predictable than adults in their behaviour and cannot be relied on not to run on to the road. Again, the fact that the teacher is in a position of trust and has accepted a special responsibility for the children's welfare is important; he is likely to be judged more severely if he takes advantage of his position to satisfy his own needs at the expense of his pupils. But so, too, is the bank clerk who takes advantage of his position of trust by appropriating some of the stock-in-trade of his employer.

Secondly, if to become educated is to learn to be a person, then an important part of what has to be learnt is what is morally required in the way of behaviour. Morality is learnt more by example than by precept; and it is implicit in the teaching situation that the teacher sets himself up as a model to be followed. The teacher is in effect saying: 'That is what to believe about so-and-so, it's what I believe, and these are my reasons'; or 'I think pond-life is fascinating; don't you?'; or 'this is how to hold the bat; the way I do it is the way you should.' Therefore, anything which the teacher does the children are likely to copy. If the teacher is rude or dishonest in his dealings with his pupils, they are likely to copy him in this as in other things. And, even if the teacher is primarily concerned to teach arithmetic or geography rather than how to behave morally, he should at least avoid having a bad effect on his pupils' moral education.

These remarks leave open the possibility of a more positive role for the teacher in relation to moral education. The subject of moral education will receive more detailed consideration in the volume devoted to ethics in this series.

SUMMARY

1. Teachers help others to learn and teaching is what they do in providing such help.

2. Teaching consists of actions, in the technical philosophical sense, which form a pattern of activity.

3. Teaching is a goal-directed activity; the relevant goal is the bringing about of learning.

4. Success in teaching, therefore, will depend on having a clear idea of what it is hoped to achieve; that is, a precise idea of just what learning it is hoped to bring about. For older children, whose studies are structured by the curriculum, this is less difficult than for young children. Assessment of teaching methods can be made only if the point of using them is understood. Knowledge of the needs of children is also important for successful teaching.

5. The criteria of success in learning are internal to the material which has to be learnt; they cannot be supplied arbitrarily by the teacher. Nevertheless, there is room for differences in the standards applied.

6. 'Teaching' is not the name of a method of doing anything; it is not, therefore, the name of a rational method of doing anything. Teaching is to be contrasted with advertising, propaganda and indoctrination.

7. The relationship between a teacher and a pupil is governed by the same moral considerations which govern all social interactions. The teacher has also a special responsibility for the moral education of the child.

FURTHER READING

1. On the connection between education and values see chapter 5, section 8 (pages 69–71) and references for that section. On the account which I have given, not everything which a person is taught contributes to his education.

2. Actions are also discussed in chapter 5, sections 6 and 7 (page 66). Chapter 6, section 2 (page 79) and following are also relevant. On actions as forming a pattern, see Hart (chapter 3 in 67). The restriction placed on the possibilities of action open to us by our concepts is probably best brought out by a historical example; before the invention of germ theory, for example, a doctor could not disinfect a wound or instruments against the possibility of infection by germs. See chapter 5, section 1 of Winch (106). Winch's discussion of voting in chapter 2, section 2 also develops this point. The whole of chapters 2 and 5 of Winch is relevant.

In a similar way, the experiences open to us are limited by the concepts we have. This includes the possibility of experiencing emotions. (On emotions, see Bedford in (26) and Peters (120)). One cannot be envious of the property of another, for example, without having some conception of personal property; or feel guilty without some idea of what it is to do wrong.   This argument applies even to the seemingly basic emotion of fear. To be afraid of something is to see it as offering a threat to oneself. To attribute fear to a new-born baby is to presuppose that it has a conception of itself as distinct from its environment and that it is able to see in present circumstances the possibility of future harm to itself. There is, therefore, an oddity of talking of birth as a traumatic experience. An adult trying to escape from a dark confined space through a narrow fluid-filled passage, and being battered and bruised in the process, would feel certain emotions. But this is no reason for supposing that the child has similar experiences in being born. There may, of course, be a connection of a causal kind between difficult births and later personality difficulties. But nothing like the memory of that birth could function as a reason, conscious or unconscious, for any later behaviour. I could not possibly remember an experience which I did not have; and being born is not an experience in the relevant sense at all. It is not conceptually structured in the way in which the experience of an adult in similar circumstances would be.

3. Cf. the discussion of the aims of education in chapter 4 (pages 49–53).

4. On the concept of need, see Peters (70, especially pages 17/18). There is, of course, an increasing emphasis on the importance of the acquisition of concepts, especially in discussions of the education of young children, partly as a result of the developmental studies of Piaget. The importance of language is being studied by Basil Bernstein at the London Institute of Education.

5. Cf. sections 8, 9 and 10 of chapter 7 (pages 101–6). The examinations for the Certificate of Secondary Education, Mode III, are set separately for each school by the teachers in the school, allowing them to decide themselves whether what they hoped would be learnt has been learnt. As in all cases of internal assessment, an external check is a necessary safeguard.

6. For Scheffler's views on 'teaching' see Scheffler (87, chapters 4 and 5; and 86, chapter 1).

7. See Williams (chapter 6 in 51) and Peters (72, chapter 8).

9 Teachers

1 TEACHING AS A PROFESSION

So far I have been talking about 'teaching' rather than 'teachers'. And it is sometimes assumed that once we are clear about what 'teaching' is, 'a teacher' can be defined briefly as one who teaches. But though brevity is always a virtue, this is too brief. Teaching is a profession and not everybody who teaches is a member of that profession. Teaching occurs when one person accepts responsibility for the learning of another, but in not every case is the acceptance of that responsibility formal and explicit.

An analogy may make this clearer. It would be a perfectly proper use of the word 'nurse' to call somebody a nurse because she has looked after a sick person. The word 'nurse' is then being used descriptively; the person described has been engaged in the sort of activity in which nurses typically engage. She has mopped the patient's brow and taken his temperature and generally done whatever she could to bring about his return to health. In the same way, to call someone a teacher may be simply to imply that he has been engaged in the activity of teaching. And if that is all, then we can understand what is being said, provided we know what teaching is.

But more often this is not all that is being said when someone is described as a nurse or a teacher. Usually we mean by a nurse someone who brings special skill and knowledge to the job of nursing and whose competence has been publicly recognised by the award of certain qualifications. A teacher also is one whose special knowledge of his subject and of children make him competent to teach and who has been granted a certificate of competence. Such competence is not gained overnight or without effort or by chance; it is gained painfully, over a period of time, and with the intention of using it *as* a nurse or teacher. And by a nurse or teacher we usually mean someone who is not only equipped for a particular job, but someone who does that job and gets paid for it.

A teacher, therefore, is not just someone who does teach, but someone whose job it is to teach; someone who has not only accepted responsibility for the learning of others, but has done so explicitly. Responsibility for education is not confined to the teacher; the government, local authorities, school managers and governors all have responsibilities in the field of education. But they discharge their responsibility by seeing that school buildings are provided, by laying down standards and by employing teachers. And the teacher is the one who is responsible for doing the actual teaching.

2 TEACHERS AND SCHOOLS

I have already pointed out that the scope for speaking of education at all exists only if we assume a social context and that a great deal of education consists in something like catching up on man's social evolution. And teaching is itself a particular social phenomenon and, therefore, the relationship between teacher and taught is governed by the moral considerations relevant to any relationship between members of a human society. Now I want to look at the social situation created when that relationship becomes formalised or institutionalised; that is, when some individuals occupy the role of teachers, and others the role of pupils, within recognisable social institutions.

It is obvious that it is in schools that the members of a social group can be clearly assigned to one of the two roles of teacher or taught. What is not so obvious is just what a school is. Certainly a school is not to be confused with a school building; a building, that is, at which teaching takes place. Of course, it will be convenient to have a building in which to teach, with walls and a roof to keep out the cold and rain and the heat of the sun, and classrooms containing tables and chairs and books; but these things are not essential. In a poor country with a warm climate there may be no building at all; the school may simply meet under the shade of a convenient tree. In short, what is important about schools is that they are social institutions, not that they are buildings. What then is a social institution?

Social institutions owe their existence to the social rules which govern them. Social rules are of a logically different kind from causal laws; the most important difference being that a person governed by a social law has a choice about whether to follow the rule or law. By contrast, it makes no sense to say that, though falling bodies (human as well as others) are governed by the law of gravity, a particular falling body is not accelerating at the rate of thirty-two feet per second because it decided to fall at some other rate, or not to fall at all.

It is important to note that social rules are not all of a kind. Some are legal, some moral, and others adopted simply for convenience in a particular context. So, though a person governed by a social rule always has a choice about whether to obey the rule, he does not always have a choice about whether to be subject to the rule. There is a sense in which I am free to steal or kill, even though to do so is to break the law of the land; what I am not free to do is to exempt myself from the law which forbids such actions – it is no defence to a charge of murder to say you don't accept the law forbidding murder as binding upon you. By contrast, some social rules, like those of a social or sports club, apply only to those who have chosen to join the club.

Children become members of those social institutions which we call schools because they, and their parents, are subject to the law of the land, which says that children must go to school whether they like it or not. Teachers, on the other hand, are teachers because they have chosen to earn their living as teachers and have accepted posts at schools or with local authorities. And the rules operate to structure the social situation in which teachers and pupils meet, ascribing to some the role of teachers and to others the role of pupils. A school viewed as a social institution rather than as a building owes its identity to a set of social rules, which are accepted voluntarily by some of those to whom they apply and are imposed on others. The rules operate to structure the situation in which teaching takes place, creating the roles of teacher and pupil, and have as their overriding purpose the creation of a social situation in which education can be brought about.

To accept the role of a teacher in such an institution is to accept responsibility for bringing about the required learning; it is also to be authorised, within limits, to do what is necessary to discharge that responsibility effectively.

3   RESPONSIBILITY AND THE TEACHER

The teacher's job is to teach, and teaching is an activity which can be carried on successfully or unsuccessfully. Suppose there are grounds for saying that a teacher has been unsuccessful in his teaching on a particular occasion. Is he entitled to shrug his shoulders and say: 'Too bad, but that's how it is. I'm a teacher, and "teaching" is a task word and not an achievement word'?

Obviously not. The question of teaching only arises when it is reasonable to suppose that something can be done to help bring about learning by someone; so at least the possibility of success is a presupposition of the teaching situation. Moreover, a teacher is not just one who does try to bring about learning, but one who has accepted responsibility for bringing it about. He will, therefore, be held responsible for failure to do so.

The situation is, therefore, typical of all those in which somebody is regarded as responsible for doing something. In general, people are held responsible for what they should have done, but haven't; as in the case of the teacher who ought to have been instrumental in bringing about learning but wasn't. And also for what they have done, but ought not to have done; as, for example, when the Knave of Hearts stole some tarts, or Tom stole a pig. And to say that someone is responsible for what they did or failed to do is at least to say that they will be held accountable for their action. It will be appropriate to ask for an explanation of the lapse and, if no satisfactory explanation is forthcoming, to censure them for it.

It is important to note that a satisfactory explanation may be forthcoming. Tom may say that he stole the pig because his wife and ten children were starving, and this will at least put the matter in a different light. Or he may say that, coming home from the

Rose and Crown about the hour of dusk, he mistook the pig for his wife and tucked her under his arm in a spirit of pure affection; he didn't really steal the pig, in other words. But not any explanation will excuse blame. The Knave of Hearts may say that he was feeling peckish when he saw the tarts, and why shouldn't he take them if he wanted to? In that case his explanation will not count as a justification of what he did.

So the teacher whose pupils fail to learn has at least some explaining to do. The reason may be that he was lazy or incompetent; these are at least possible explanations. But the teacher has as much right as anyone else to have his professional integrity and competence taken for granted, assuming, that is, that he is professionally qualified. In general, students do not have a responsibility for their own learning, as the teacher has for seeing that they learn. This is obvious enough in the kindergarten, though for those who accept a place at a college of education or university the position is very different. But though it is the teacher rather than the student who is responsible for the student's learning, the teacher cannot do the student's learning for him. Children may lack motivation; which is equivalent to saying that they are lazy except that it lacks the censorious tone. Of course, it might be said that it is up to the teacher to provide the motivation, but that is not quite as easy as providing pencils and paper. Lack of motivation may spring from deep-rooted personality traits, or reflect current home circumstances, and the extent to which it is possible to compensate for these in the class room is limited. Or children may be dull – that is, incompetent learners. Again, it might be said that the teacher should not set out to teach a child what is beyond its capacity to learn. But it is difficult to avoid doing so when trying to cope simultaneously with forty-odd children, and in any case some things, like learning to read, are so important that the effort must be made, whatever the ability of the child. And often the teacher is bound by examination requirements or even by the standards laid down by a grade system.

In short, though the teacher *is* responsible for seeing that learning occurs, his success or failure in bringing it about is only partly dependent on factors within his control. Of course, part of the professional training of teachers consists of getting them to accept that responsibility, but they should at the same time be brought to realise that their efforts may fail due to factors beyond their control; lack of success will not then provide proper grounds for blame from others or for self-generated feelings of guilt.

4 AUTHORITY AND THE TEACHER

In general, the only rational answer to the question 'Why do you believe that?' is a reference to the evidence for accepting the belief as true. And similarly the only rational answer to the question 'Why did you do that?' contains a reference to good reasons for doing that. Of course, people's beliefs and actions are often irrational; but in that case, though they may be subject to explanation, the question of justification will not arise. In general, therefore, it is not a good reason for believing that something is the case simply because somebody has said that it is, any more than it is a good reason for doing something simply because somebody has told you to do it. 'Would you have stuck your finger in the fire if Johnny had told you to?' is obviously a question expecting the answer 'No'. In general 'He told me so' or 'He told me to do it' do not point to good grounds for believing or doing anything, though they may provide an explanation of why something was done or believed. I now wish to qualify this position.

'He told me so' is a good answer to the question 'Why do you believe that?' when 'he' is an authority in the area to which the belief belongs; and 'He told me to do it' is a good answer to the question when 'he' is in authority over me. It is part of the qualifications required for acceptance in the role of a teacher that the teacher is an authority in the field in which he is to teach. And you cannot offer to accept responsibility for bringing about learning in a particular field without committing yourself to a claim to competence in that field. Of course, the phrase 'an authority' is usually reserved for one whose special competence in a field is recognised by his fellow-workers in that field; so a recognised authority in physics or psychology is one whose views in those subjects are recognised by other physicists or psychologists as worthy of consideration because they come from him. And the teacher of physics or psychology is not usually an authority in his subject in this sense. What he is committed to claiming is to be an authority in his subject relative to those whom he teaches. The teacher is an authority for his pupils in the sense that they have the right to look to him for reliable guidance as to which beliefs are true and which methods of establishing truth are acceptable, within his subject. The teacher has not so much the right to lay down what shall be believed, as the duty to offer for acceptance those beliefs and only those beliefs which are worthy of being believed.

So the teacher is an authority in relation to the particular discipline which he teaches. And he is also *in authority* in the social group which constitutes the class or teaching unit. He is in authority in the sense that he is authorised, that is he has the right, to take what steps are necessary to see that his teaching is effective. However reliable the teacher's knowledge of his subject, and however carefully he presents his material, his pupils will not learn anything unless they listen to what he has to say. He is, therefore, authorised to do what is necessary to see that they do listen; if he is without authority in this sense he will be lucky if he gets much attention. Of course, his authority may be limited; as, for example, there was once a law which forbade a man to beat his wife with a stick of more than an inch in diameter.

An important question which arises here is what gives a man the right to impose his will on others in this way. 'Authority' has most often been discussed in its political context. Political authority is the right of the government to make laws and decisions; it occupies the opposite face of the coin to political obligation, to which I referred briefly in chapter four, section two (page 59). But the teacher's authority – and that of the husband too, if he still has any – cannot be understood simply by analogy with the political case. The teacher's authority comes to him simply by virtue of the role which he occupies and is related to the purpose of the social institution in which that role occurs. The teacher is in authority because he has been placed in authority by the local authority or board of governors, or whoever it is that has the authority to make such appointments. If we then raise the question of their right to give such authority, again a fairly straightforward answer is available; the authority was vested in them by statute. And if that authority in turn is questioned, one gets back to the question of political authority. But the source of political authority cannot in turn derive from a higher authority, because there is no higher authority, at least in the obvious sense with which I have been concerned so far.

A teacher who is in authority has the right to be obeyed by those over whom he has authority. The important word here is 'right', for two reasons. Firstly, the fact that someone is in authority over me is in itself a good reason why I should do what they tell me to do; 'authority' is a moral notion, to be contrasted with mere power. It is right to obey one in authority, not merely expedient to do so. Secondly, however, it does not follow from the fact that someone is in authority and therefore has the *right* to be obeyed, that they will in fact be obeyed. The fact that children do not recognise a teacher's authority does not mean that he is not in authority; since his authority comes not from them but from those to whom he owes his appointment. But it does mean that if he is to be obeyed he will have to rely on something other than the mere fact that he is in authority. Indeed, not only does the teacher have the right to insist on being obeyed; he also has the duty to do so. 'Authority' is not therefore to be contrasted with 'force', as it is to be contrasted with (mere) 'power'. On the contrary, the use of force is a perfectly proper exercise of authority. Just as there are moral objections to the adoption of certain teaching methods, so too there may be moral objections to certain ways of asserting authority, and one might object to the use of fear in the classroom, just as one might object to the Bloody Assize of Judge Jefferies. But the objection is not that this is not an exercise of authority, but that it is a morally objectionable way of exercising it.

I think it is worth returning for a moment to the political case and the question of the ultimate source of political authority. Hobbes' answer was, in effect, that there is no difference between authority and power at this level, but it is not an answer which I find acceptable. I prefer the answer of Locke and Rousseau, that the source of political authority lies in the consent of those over whom it is exercised. The teacher is in authority whether he is obeyed or not, since his authority comes from above. But in the case of the supreme authority, there is no one above (this is what is *meant* by sovereign authority); therefore, if the distinction between authority and power is to be maintained, the source of authority can only come from below. Of course, there are problems about the way consent is to be expressed, and about the rights of majorities over minorities, and so on. My point is simply that at the level of political authority there is only one source of authority, i.e. consent; whereas at lower levels there are two sources, consent and authorisation from a higher authority. And what is important in the teaching situation is the latter and not the former.

It is in this sense that I think a school is an essentially authoritarian institution. I think it must be because the teacher, in addition to being an authority on an area of belief in the way I indicated earlier in this section, is also an authority on ways of behaving. The responsible teacher has very definite ideas on what sort of social institution he wants the school he teaches in to be. He wants it to be one in which courtesy and consideration for others, for example, play a part, rather than one dominated by rudeness and bullying. In the political case, authority is exercised over those who are presumed to be adults, competent to form their own judgements about what sort of life they want to live. In the school the situation is different; authority is exercised over those who are not yet adult and an important aspect of education is helping them to come to value a particular mode of social life.

Having stressed the sense in which I think a school is essentially an authoritarian institution, however, I ought to point out that this still leaves room for the contrast which is often made between authoritarian and democratic forms of schooling. It would be consistent with what I have said to adopt, as an educational ideal, the view that a school should, so far as possible, be a community which is bound together by common acceptance of a set of rules, rather than by a set of rules imposed in an authoritarian way by the teachers on the children. There is plenty of scope in schools for behaviour to be governed by the notion of 'That's the way we do things here', rather than by that of 'If we don't obey the teachers and the rules they lay down we will be punished'.

5 THE PUPIL—TEACHER RELATIONSHIP

I have tried to say a little about the way in which the relationship between the teacher and his pupils is structured in those social institutions which we call 'schools'. There are other social relationships which are structured or formalised in our society in the same sort of way; for example, the relationship between employer and employee, or citizen and government official. The most obvious one to compare with the pupil–teacher relationship, however, is that which exists between the parents and their children in the family. The only point I wish to make here is that it would be a mistake to suppose that the attitudes and emotions which are appropriate in the one situation are necessarily also appropriate in the other. For example, one may wish to say that the appropriate attitude of a parent to a child should be one of love; it does not follow that a similar attitude is appropriate on the part of the teacher to his pupils. 'Love' is a word which is used very loosely, but at least one might suggest that it has notions like permanence and partiality built in. Perhaps, therefore, the appropriate attitude of a teacher towards his pupils should be something more like 'affection' than 'love'. Most teachers do not concern themselves with their pupils' academic progress only; though, as teachers, this must be their primary concern. But the teacher cannot, and should not, replace the parent, and his attitude to his pupils should reflect the necessarily temporary nature of their relationship.

6 UNIVERSITIES

In chapter 1 I suggested that education could best be thought of as an activity of a practical kind; one, that is, which aimed at a practical result. In the case of education, the aim is that someone should learn something; in other words, education is concerned with the transmission of knowledge and is, therefore, to be contrasted with theoretical activities which have as their aim the acquisition of new knowledge.

Universities, however, present something of a problem in this connection; since, though they are obviously educational institutions, they do not confine themselves to the transmission of knowledge, but also concern themselves with the acquisition of new knowledge. And this has led to disagreement as to whether their primary function is the transmission or the acquisition of knowledge.

What is distinctive of teaching to final honours standards is that it attempts to bring the student to the frontiers of knowledge in his subject. The student is given an opportunity of reaching a position which will at least make it possible for him to take part himself in the extension of knowledge in his subject. But such an opportunity can only be offered by those who are themselves active in research in their subject. The division of labour, which works satisfactorily elsewhere in the educational system, between those who transmit knowledge and those who gain new knowledge, breaks down at this level. Teaching at university level can only be undertaken by those who are also active in theoretical research in the subject.

SUMMARY

1. A teacher is one who has explicitly accepted responsibility for the learning of others.

2. Most teaching takes place in schools. Schools are social institutions, owing their existence to the social rules which govern them. The rules lay down the duties which it is the responsibility of the teacher to carry out and also give him the necessary authority for doing so.

3. The teacher will, therefore, be held responsible if learning fails to take place and may be asked for an explanation of the failure. It does not follow that a satisfactory explanation may not be forthcoming.

4. The teacher's knowledge of his subject makes him an authority on it, relative to his pupils. He is also in authority in the social group which constitutes the class. The teacher's authority does not come to him from those over whom it is exercised, but is given to him from a higher authority. Therefore, though it gives him the right to be obeyed, it does not follow that he will in fact be obeyed. Though the school is basically an authoritarian institution, there remains scope for the pupils to set up and adopt their own standards.

5. The relationship between the teacher and the pupil is more appropriately one of affection rather than of love.

K

6. It is part of the idea of a university that the same people should undertake responsibility for both teaching and research.

FURTHER READING

1. See Bradley on 'My station and its duties' in Bradley (21, chapter 5).

2. See chapter 5, section 2 (pages 59–60) on the social context of education, chapter 5, section 4 (page 63) on social rules; and references for those sections.

3. On responsibility, see Hart (chapter 8 in 32) and Austin (chapter 3 in 27).

4. On authority see Peters (119) and Winch (122); Peters' views are more easily available in Benn and Peters (15, chapter 14). See also Peters (72, chapter 9).

The views of Locke, Hobbes and Rousseau on the source of political obligation were discussed in chapter 5, section 2 (page 59).

Hart (43) has a great deal to say about the difference between accepting rules as a guide to behaviour and obeying them out of fear of the consequences of breaking them. See especially his discussion of the internal aspect of rules on pages 86–8 and elsewhere.

6. See Griffiths (chapter 9 in 4).

Bibliography

Books

1. Aaron, R. I. *John Locke* (Oxford University Press, 2nd ed. 1955)
2. Ackermann, R. J. *Theories of Knowledge: A Critical Introduction* (McGraw-Hill 1965)
3. Alston, W. P. *Philosophy of Language* (Prentice-Hall 1964)
4. Archambault, R. D. (Ed.) *Philosophical Analysis and Education* (Routledge and Kegan Paul 1965)
5. Aristotle *Politics* (translated E. Barker) (Oxford University Press 1946)
6. Austin, J. L. *Sense and Sensibilia* (Oxford University Press 1962)
7. Ayer, A. J. *The Concept of a Person* (Macmillan 1963)
8. Ayer, A. J. *Language, Truth and Logic* (Gollancz, 2nd ed. 1945)
9. Ayer, A. J. (Ed.) *Logical Positivism* (Free Press 1960)
10. Ayer, A. J. *The Problem of Knowledge* (Penguin 1956)
11. Ayer, A. J. & others *The Revolution in Philosophy* (Macmillan 1956)
12. Barker, E. *Political Thought of Plato and Aristotle* (Russell 1959)
13. Barker S. F. *Introduction to Philosophy of Mathematics* (Prentice-Hall 1964)
14. Basson, A. H. & O'Connor, D. J. *Introduction to Symbolic Logic* (University Tutorial Press 1953)
15. Benn, S. I. & Peters, R. S. *Social Principles and the Democratic State* (Allen and Unwin 1959)
16. Berofsky, B. (Ed.) *Freedom and Determinism* (Harper Row 1966)
17. Black, M. *Companion to Wittgenstein's Tractatus* (Cambridge University Press 1964)
18. Black, M. (Ed.) *The Importance of Language* (Prentice-Hall 1962)
19. Black, M. *Models and Metaphors* (Cornell University Press 1962)
20. Bradley, F. H. *Appearance and Reality* (Oxford University Press 1893)
21. Bradley, F. H. *Ethical Studies* (Oxford University Press 1962) (1st ed. 1876)
22. Bradley, F. H. *Principles of Logic* (Oxford University Press, 2nd ed. 1922)

23. Braithwaite, R. B. *Scientific Explanation* (Cambridge University Press 1955)

24. Braybrooke, D. (Ed.) *Philosophical Problems of the Social Sciences* (Macmillan, N.Y. 1965)

25. Brown, J. A. C. *Techniques of Persuasion* (Pelican 1963)

26. Chappell, V. C. (Ed.) *The Philosophy of Mind* (Prentice-Hall 1962)

27. Chappell, V. C. (Ed.) *Ordinary Language* (Prentice-Hall 1964)

28. Chisholm, R. M. *Theory of Knowledge* (Prentice-Hall 1966)

29. Cross, R. C. & Woozley, A. D. *Plato's Republic: A Philosophical Commentary* (Macmillan 1964)

30. Dray, W. H. *Philosophy of History* (Prentice-Hall 1964)

31. Flew, A. G. N. (Ed.) *Essays in Conceptual Analysis* (Macmillan 1956)

32. Flew, A. G. N. (Ed.) *Logic and Language*, 1st series (Blackwell 1951)

33. Flew, A. G. N. (Ed.) *Logic and Language*, 2nd series (Blackwell 1953)

34. Gardiner, P. (Ed.) *The Nature of Historical Explanation* (Oxford 1952)

35. Geach, P. *Mental Acts* (Routledge & Kegan Paul 1957)

36. Gibson, Q. *The Logic of Social Enquiry* (Routledge 1960)

37. Gough, J. W. *The Social Contract* (Oxford 1936)

38. Gustavson, D. F. (Ed.) *Essays in Philosophical Psychology* (New York, Doubleday & Co. 1964)

39. Hamlyn, D. W. *The Psychology of Perception* (Routledge & Kegan Paul 1957)

40. Hanson, N. R. *Patterns of Discovery* (Cambridge University Press 1958)

41. Hare, R. M. *The Language of Morals* (Oxford University Press 1952)

42. Harré, R. *An Introduction to Logic of the Sciences* (Macmillan 1960)

43. Hart, H. L. A. *The Concept of Law* (Oxford University Press 1961)

44. Hilgard, E. R. *Theories of Learning* (Methuen 1948)

45. Hobbes, T. *Leviathan* (ed. M. Oakeshott) (Blackwell 1946)

46. Hollins, T. H. B. (Ed.) *Aims in Education* (Manchester University Press 1964)

47. Hook S. (Ed.) *Determinism and Freedom* (Collier Books 1961)

48. Hospers J. *An Introduction to Philosophical Analysis* (Routledge & Kegan Paul 1956)

49. Kneale, W. *Probability and Induction* (Oxford University Press 1949)

50. Laslett, P. (Ed.) *Philosophy, Politics and Society* 1st series (Blackwell 1956)

51. Laslett, P. & Runciman, W. G. (Eds.) *Philosophy, Politics and Society*, 2nd series (Blackwell 1962)

52. Locke, J. *The Second Treatise of Government* (ed. J. W. Gough) (Blackwell 1946)

53. Marsh, R. C. (Ed.) *Logic and Knowledge* (Allen & Unwin 1956)

54. Mill, J. S. *System of Logic* (Longmans 1898)

55. Mill, J. S. *Utilitarianism, Liberty and Representative Government* (Dent (Everyman) 1910)

56. Moore, G. E. *Philosophical Papers* (Allen & Unwin 1959)

57. Moore, G. E. *Principia Ethica* (Cambridge 1903, Paperback 1959)

58. Morris, C. *Signs, Language and Behaviour* (Prentice-Hall 1946)

59. Oakeshott, M. *Rationalism in Politics and Other Essays* (Methuen 1962)

60. O'Connor, D. J. (Ed.) *A Critical History of Western Philosophy* (Collier-Macmillan 1964)

61. O'Connor, D. J. *An Introduction to the Philosophy of Education* (Routledge & Kegan Paul 1957)

62. O'Connor, D. J. *John Locke* (Penguin 1952; Dover 1967)

63. Osgood, C. E. *Method and Theory in Experimental Psychology* (Oxford University Press 1953)

64. Pap, A. *An Introduction to the Philosophy of Science* (Eyre & Spottiswoode 1963)

65. Passmore, J. *A Hundred Years of Philosophy* (Duckworth 1957)

66. Passmore, J. *Philosophical Reasoning* (Duckworth 1961)

67. Pears, D. F. (Ed.) *Freedom and the Will* (Macmillan 1963)

68. Pears, D. F. (Ed.) *The Nature of Metaphysics* (Macmillan 1957)

69. Peters, R. S. (Ed.) *The Concept of Education* (Routledge & Kegan Paul 1967)

70. Peters, R. S. *The Concept of Motivation* (Routledge & Kegan Paul 1958)

71. Peters, R. S. *Education as Initiation* (Evans Brothers 1964)

72. Peters, R. S. *Ethics and Education* (Allen & Unwin 1966)

73. Plato *The Republic*, Translated by Cornford (Oxford University Press 1941)

74. Pitcher, G. *The Philosophy of Wittgenstein* (Prentice-Hall 1964)

75. Pitcher, G. (Ed.) *Truth* (Prentice-Hall 1964)

76. Popper, K. R. *The Open Society and its Enemies* (Routledge & Kegan Paul 1945)

77. Popper, K. R. *Conjectures and Refutations* (Routledge & Kegan Paul 1963)

78. Plamenatz, J. *Man and Society* (Longmans 1963)

79. Powell, B. *Knowledge of Actions* (Allen & Unwin 1967)

80 Price, H. H. *Thinking and Experience* (Hutchinson's University Library 1953)

81. Rousseau, J. J. *The Social Contract and Discourses* (translated by G. D. H. Cole) (Dent 1913)

82. Russell, B. *Our Knowledge of the External World as a Field for Scientific Method in Philosophy* (Allen & Unwin 1914)

83. Ryle, G. *The Concept of Mind* (Hutchinson 1949)

84. Sabine, G. H. *A History of Political Theory* (Harrap 1937)

85. Sargant, W. *Battle for the Mind* (Pan 1957)

86. Scheffler, I. *Conditions of Knowledge* (Scott, Foresman & Co. 1965)

87. Scheffler, I. *The Language of Education* (Charles C. Thomas 1962)

88. Skinner, B. F. *The Behaviour of Organisms* (Appleton-Century-Crofts 1938)

89. Skinner, B. F. *Science and Human Behaviour* (Macmillan, N.Y. 1953)

90. Skinner, B. F. *Verbal Behaviour* (Appleton-Century-Crofts 1957)

91. Skinner, B. F. *Walden Two* (Macmillan, N.Y. 1948)

92. Smart, J. J. C. *Philosophy and Scientific Realism* (Routledge & Kegan Paul 1963)

93. Stevenson, C. L. *Facts and Values* (Yale 1963)

94. Strawson, P. F. *Individuals: An Essay in Descriptive Metaphysics* (Methuen 1959)

95. Thorpe, W. H. *Learning and Instinct in Animals* (Methuen 1956)

96. Tinbergen, N. *The Study of Instinct* (Oxford University Press 1951)

97. Toulmin, S. E. *The Philosophy of Science* (Hutchinson 1960)

98. Urmson, J. O. *Philosophical Analysis* (Oxford University Press 1956)

99. Vesey, G. N. A. (Ed.) *Body and Mind* (Allen & Unwin 1964)

100. Vesey, G. N. A. *The Embodied Mind* (Allen & Unwin 1965)

101. Walsh, W. H. *An Introduction to Philosophy of History* (Hutchinson 1951)

102. Walsh, W. H. *Metaphysics* (Hutchinson 1963)

103. Warnock, G. J. *English Philosophy since 1900* (Oxford University Press 1958)

104. Weldon, T. D. *The Vocabulary of Politics* (Penguin 1953)

105. Whitehead, A. N. *The Aims of Education and Other Essays* (Benn 1962)

106. Winch, P. *The Idea of a Social Science* (Routledge & Kegan Paul 1958)

107. Wittgenstein, L. *Philosophical Investigations* (Blackwell 1958)

108. Wittgenstein, L. *Tractatus Logico-Philosophicus* (translated by D. F. Pears and B. F. McGuinness) (Routledge & Kegan Paul 1961)

109. Woozley A. D. *Theory of Knowledge* (Hutchinson 1949)

Articles

110. Anderson, J. 'Art and Morality', *Australasian Journal of Philosophy and Psychology*, **21** (June 1943)

111. Barrett, C. 'Concepts and Concept Formation', *Proceedings of the Aristotelian Society*, **63** (1962/3)

112. Chisholm, R. M. 'Sentences about Believing', *Proceedings of the Aristotelian Society*, **56** (1955/56)

113. Griffiths, A. P. 'Formulating Moral Principles', *Mind* (1956)

114. Griffiths, A. P. 'On Belief', *Proceedings of the Aristotelian Society*, **63** (1962/3)

115. Hirst, P. H. 'Philosophy and Educational Theory', *British Journal of Educational Studies* (November 1963)

116. Lucas, J. R. 'On Not Worshipping Facts', *Philosophical Quarterly* (1958)

117. MacCorquodale, K. & Meehl, P. E. 'On a Distinction between Hypothetical Constructs and Intervening Variables', *Psychological Review* (1948)

118. O'Connor, D. J. 'Possibility and Choice', *Proceedings of the Aristotelian Society*, **34** (1960)

119. Peters, R. S. 'Authority', *Proceedings of the Aristotelian Society* Suppl., **32** (1958)

120. Peters, R. S. 'Emotions and the Category of Passivity', *Proceedings of the Aristotelian Society*, **62** (1961/62)

121. Phillips, D. Z. & Mounce, H. O. 'On Morality's Having a Point', *Philosophy* (1965)

122. Winch, P. 'Authority', *Proceedings of the Aristotelian Society* Suppl., **32** (1958)

123. Winch, P. 'Nature and Convention', *Proceedings of the Aristotelian Society*, **60** (1959/60)

124. Winch. P. 'Understanding a Primitive Society', *American Philosophical Quarterly* (October 1964)

Glossary

ACHIEVEMENT WORD. A word that indicates that someone has succeeded in doing something, e.g. has won a race. (Cf. task word.)

ACTIVITY. A pattern of actions linked by a common purpose.

AGENT. One capable of performing actions.

AN AUTHORITY. One whose opinions in a particular area of knowledge are accepted as a reliable guide to the truth or to the correct way to proceed, either because of an established reputation or formal qualification in that field.

A PRIORI STATEMENT. A statement the truth of which is independent of observation, e.g. the truths of geometry.

BELIEF. A conception of an aspect of the world which is accepted by the believer as accurately (or truly) reflecting the way things are.

A TRUE BELIEF is a belief which does reflect things accurately; a FALSE BELIEF one which does not.

CONCEPT. An order imposed on or seen in the world by an observer.

CONCEPTUAL SCHEME. A group of concepts capable of structuring a whole area of experience.

CONDITIONING. One way, or a number of ways, in which changes in behaviour are brought about as a result of something happening to something. 'Conditioning' is therefore the name of a process.

CONTINGENT. A statement is contingently true if its truth is dependent on non-linguistic facts, e.g. 'The world is round' is contingently true, because the world might have been flat, but as a matter of fact is round. (Cf. necessary.)

CRITERIA OF VALIDITY. The methods relied upon for distinguishing between correct and incorrect beliefs or practices within a theoretical or practical activity.

DISCOURSE. The language typical of the discussion involved in an activity (e.g. practical discourse, theoretical discourse, moral discourse, scientific discourse).

EMPIRICISM. The philosophical tradition which regards the senses (especially sight) as the ultimate source of all knowledge. (Cf. rationalism, empirical question.)

EMPIRICAL QUESTION. A question which can only be answered by observation.

EPISTEMOLOGY. The part of philosophy concerned with knowledge; including the possibility of knowledge, how it is to be attained, and what is involved in the possession of it.

EPISTEMOLOGICAL SCEPTICISM. Doubt about the possibility of ever really knowing anything.

ESTABLISHED KNOWLEDGE. Those facts discovered by a branch of enquiry which are so well supported that they are accepted by all competent to form an opinion.

ETHICS. That part of philosophy concerned with morality; especially with the language of morals and the justification of moral judgements.

'FIDO' – FIDO THEORY OF MEANING. The theory that all words which have meaning are the names of objects, just as 'Fido' is the name of the dog Fido.

FORMAL EDUCATION. Education in which two parties can be distinguished (i.e. teachers and pupils), and in which one party accepts responsibility for the education of the other. (Cf. informal education.)

FORMAL KNOWLEDGE. Knowledge structured by concepts possessed only by those members of a society who have had a special opportunity of acquiring them.

IN AUTHORITY. One who is in authority has the right to decide what is to be done in a particular social institution; his authority is related to the purpose of that institution.

INFORMAL EDUCATION. Education in which two parties cannot be distinguished. (Cf. formal education.)

KNOWLEDGE CLAIMS. Explicit claims to rational belief, made by the speaker on his own behalf or on behalf of another.

LINGUISTIC CONTEXT. The context of other words in which a word or sentence occurs. (Cf. semantic context.)

LOGIC. The branch of philosophy which concerns itself with the rules to which arguments must conform if they are valid.

METAPHYSICS. The attempt to provide a general description of the world, or of reality (as opposed to appearance).

NECESSARY. A statement is necessarily true if its truth is independent of any non-linguistic facts, e.g. 'The same object cannot at the same time be red and green all over'. (Cf. contingent.)

OSTENSIVE DEFINITION. A definition provided by pointing to examples; for example, explaining what is meant by 'vermilion' by pointing to objects of that colour.

PERSON. One who has a conception of both the physical world, as containing things related to one another by causal laws, and of the social world, as containing persons related to one another by social rules; and who has a conception of himself as a person. Persons also hold beliefs about the world, and are capable of being active in relation to it.

PHILOSOPHICAL ANALYSIS. The clarification of the meanings of words and sentences.

POSITIVISM. A movement originally opposed to the introduction of unobservables (like the atom) into science. Later (in Vienna in the nineteen twenties) the logical positivists used the newly developed logical techniques and a verification theory of meaning to reject metaphysics.

PRACTICAL ACTIVITY. An activity the point of which is to change something, e.g. politics, education, farming. (Cf. theoretical activity.)

PROPOSITIONAL FUNCTION. A formula from which a sentence can be produced by replacing the variables (indicated by letters) by appropriate words, e.g. 'X knows that p'; substitution here might give 'Esmeralda knows that snow is white'.

PROTOCOL STATEMENTS. The name given by the logical positivists to those statements which are directly verifiable (like 'This is red').

RATIONAL BELIEF. A belief held in the light of the evidence for its truth.

RATIONALISM. The philosophical tradition which emphasises the importance of reason in gaining knowledge. (Cf. empiricism, *a priori*.)

SECOND-ORDER ACTIVITY. One which concerns itself with a first-order activity, especially the discourse typical of it and the procedures implicit in it.

SEMANTIC CONTEXT. The non-linguistic context in which a word or sentence occurs. (Cf. linguistic context.)

SIGN. Anything which has been found to indicate the presence, or past or impending presence, of something else, e.g. lightning is a sign of thunder a few seconds later.

SOCIAL CONTRACT. The supposed agreement into which man entered, whereby he agreed to submit to civil authority in exchange for the benefits of society. (Cf. state of nature.)

SOLIPSISM. The view that the only conscious being, or the only conscious being I can have any contact with, is myself; connected with *idealism*, the view that the world consists only of my experiences.

SOVEREIGN AUTHORITY. Ultimate authority, not subject to any higher authority.

STATE OF NATURE. The supposed state of man before he formed societies and came to receive the benefits of social organisation. (Cf. social contract.)

STIPULATIVE DEFINITION. A statement of the meaning which the user of an expression intends to attach to it.

SYMBOL. Anything used in communication to stand for something other than itself. (Cf. sign.)

SYNONYMOUS. Two expressions are synonymous if they have the same meaning.

TASK WORD. A word which indicates that someone is trying to do something, e.g. someone who is running in a race is trying to win it. (Cf. achievement word.)

TEACHER. One who has not only accepted responsibility for the learning of another, but who has done so explicitly; who has received special training to enable him to do his job, and who gets paid for doing it.

TEACHING. Helping others to learn.

THEORETICAL ACTIVITY. An activity the point of which is to discover what is the case. (Cf. practical activity.)

UNIFIED LANGUAGE OF NATURAL SCIENCE. A language in which all meaningful propositions could be expressed. The logical positivists thought that the language of physics provided a basis for such a language.

Index